Reading the New Testament
for the First Time

Reading the New Testament for the First Time

Ronald J. Allen

William B. Eerdmans Publishing Company
Grand Rapids, Michigan / Cambridge, U.K.

Published 2012 by
Wm. B. Eerdmans Publishing Co.
2140 Oak Industrial Drive N.E., Grand Rapids, Michigan 49505 /
P.O. Box 163, Cambridge CB3 9PU U.K.

Printed in the United States of America

17 16 15 14 13 12   7 6 5 4 3 2 1

ISBN 978-0-8028-6735-3

www.eerdmans.com

Contents

Contents

Introduction

This Book Is for People Brand New to the New Testament

This book is for people who have never picked up a copy of the New Testament. To read this book, you do not have to know *anything* about the New Testament or the Christian faith. You do not have to be a believer or even someone "looking for answers." You do not have to know how to pronounce the hard words in the New Testament. All you need is a little curiosity.

Of course, you can read this book all by yourself. Or you can read and talk about it at the coffee shop with friends, or you can use it with a study group at a church. Each chapter concludes with questions for individual thought or group discussion.

As you read this book, you will want to have a copy of the New Testament beside you so that you can look up pertinent passages and read them for yourself. If you don't have a copy of the New Testament and would like a little help in choosing one, you might look at Appendix A, a little guide to different translations of the New Testament (pp. 179-81).

Why Did I Write This Book?

You might ask, "Why write such a simple book?" The answer is that over many years of teaching the New Testament in churches and in seminary (a school that prepares women and men to become ministers), I have run across a lot of people who would like to know more about the New Testament but do not know where to go for help. This book is for them.

The physical appearance of some copies of the Bible turns one off: a dark cover (often black) with gold-leaf edges and thin, onion-skin pages, with the words "Holy Bible" in solemn gold letters on the front. In hotel rooms, we still find copies of the Bible in the King James Version (published in the early 1600s) with its "thee" and "thou" and other archaic expressions. People are sometimes reluctant to pick up such a book because they feel that it is almost too holy to handle. For some it simply seems hopelessly out of date.

Many of the new versions of the Bible look and sound more at home in the early twenty-first century, but when you open the cover you still encounter names and places that are strange and uncommon. Several new Christians have told me that they wanted to read the Bible, but after a few days they just couldn't figure out what was going on. At the same time, few churches offer truly *basic* Bible studies. Many published Bible study resources presume a working knowledge of the Bible.

I had a poignant conversation when I was a guest Bible teacher in a church congregation. We had done a quick survey of the New Testament. After nearly all the participants had left, a woman told me quietly that she had become a Christian only a few months before. Wanting to grow in her faith, she had gone to a mid-week Bible study. She did not understand what the group was talking about, and, worse, the leading members of the group treated her like a third-class citizen. "I felt like I had to be an expert just to be there," she said. She never went back. I wonder how common her experience might be.

During services of worship, when the Bible reader announces the passage that is the basis of the sermon and invites people to turn to it in their Bibles, I often notice people flipping the Bible's pages back and forth as they try to find it.

This book provides enough hands-on information for you to feel confident to begin personal or group Bible study. After you read this book, you should be able to find passages in the New Testament and to understand them in the larger world of the New Testament. I also hope this volume will spark congregations to create Bible study groups that meet people at their level of readiness for interacting with the Bible.

An Informal Tone

My writing style in this volume is rather informal. For example, I frequently address you directly as "you." I try to write in a conversational style, avoiding technical language (or explaining such language when I have to use it). Such a relaxed approach is unusual in a book about the Bible, but I hope that makes these pages friendly and readable.

I try to follow a straightforward rule: I explain everything that may be unfamiliar or that may have a special meaning. I try to take nothing for granted as far as your knowledge of the New Testament is concerned. If you have a question in this regard, do not hesitate to email me at ron.allen@cts.edu.

Just the Facts, Ma'am

I was ten years old when our household got our first television set. *Dragnet* with Sergeant Friday was one of the most popular detective shows. When Friday interviewed a witness, the witness would sometimes accuse a particular person of committing the crime even though the witness had not actually seen the criminal activity. Sergeant Friday would say, "Just the facts, ma'am." That is, "Just tell me what you actually saw."

This book takes a "Just the facts, ma'am" approach. Of course, in the early twenty-first century we are increasingly aware that *all* awareness contains elements of interpretation. We never really perceive "just the facts." People interpret the New Testament in different ways. Scholars disagree on "the facts" themselves. Nevertheless, my aim is basic: to describe what is in the New Testament and how people in the ancient world would have understood it.

My aim is basic: to describe what is in the New Testament and how people in the ancient world would have understood it.

I keep in mind this key question, *"What does each part of the New Testament invite people to believe and to do?"* We first want to know what a passage asked its first readers to believe and to do. Only then can we see if we can apply it to ourselves today. But first we need the facts. In Chapter 13 I will reflect on how to draw on the New Testament for guidance today.

What Will You Find in
Reading the New Testament for the First Time?

Here are the contents of this book.

- Chapter 1 helps you find your way around the New Testament itself, what you will discover when you open it, and how to make your way around in it.
- Chapter 2 sketches the world of the New Testament — the larger Roman Empire and the more immediate settings in Judaism.
- Chapter 3 surveys the story of the New Testament in two different ways: (1) in the order of the main characters and events, and (2) in the order in which the books of the New Testament were written.
- Chapter 4 outlines what we can say about the story of Jesus.
- Chapter 5 overviews the life of the early church after Jesus.
- Chapter 6 focuses on Paul, one of the most famous followers of Jesus in the ancient world.

- Chapter 7 summarizes Paul's letters (Romans, 1 and 2 Corinthians,[1] Galatians, Philippians, 1 Thessalonians, and Philemon).
- Chapter 8 turns to how the Gospels of Matthew, Mark, Luke, and John tell the story of Jesus after the Romans destroyed the temple in Jerusalem. Here we will also look at the book of the Acts of the Apostles when we discuss Luke. These two books form two halves of the story of the early church, the story of Jesus (in the Gospel of Luke) and the story of his first followers after Jesus leaves the scene (in the book of Acts).
- Chapter 9 explores the letters written by students of Paul (Ephesians, Colossians, 2 Thessalonians, 1 and 2 Timothy, and Titus).
- Chapter 10 is a whirlwind tour of the other letters and books in the New Testament (Hebrews, James, 1 and 2 Peter, 1, 2, 3 John, Jude, and Revelation).
- Chapter 11 draws out some of the big ideas in the New Testament, such as love, the Realm of God, and righteousness.
- Chapter 12 catalogs some of the most famous passages in the New Testament, such as John 3:16, the Good Samaritan, and the faith chapter (Hebrews 11).
- Chapter 13 offers a simple way to use the New Testament when thinking about religious issues today.
- Appendix A reviews several popular Bible translations and what you gain and lose with each.
- Appendix B lists resources for further study of the New Testament so that you can take the next steps in getting acquainted with the Bible.

---

1. 1 Corinthians is one book in the New Testament. 2 Corinthians is another book. They are closely related. In North America we speak of them as "First Corinthians and Second Corinthians" or "First and Second Corinthians." In some other parts of the world, people say "One Corinthians and Two Corinthians." In an earlier time, the numbers were written as Roman numerals, thus: I Corinthians and II Corinthians. Other enumerated books in the New Testament follow the same pattern: 1 and 2 Thessalonians, 1 and 2 Timothy, 1 and 2 Peter, 1, 2, and 3 John. The same is true in the Old Testament: 1 and 2 Samuel, 1 and 2 Kings, 1 and 2 Chronicles.

- Appendix C sets out three ways to read the entire New Testament for yourself.
- Appendix D is an essay that questions whether we should continue to speak of the "Old Testament" and the "New Testament" or to use other language for these parts of the Bible.

This Book Unfolds like a Spiral

Many books are written like a straight line. They start at one point and go directly to another. This book is more like a spiral. It moves from one point to another, but it returns to a previous topic to add other occasional bits and pieces of information. It circles back on itself even as it moves forward. I hope this review process will help you grasp the basics of the New Testament in your mind and heart.

Bible Study Can Be Life-Giving

At its best, Bible study can be life-giving. To adapt a saying of Garrison Keillor regarding an imaginary product advertised on the radio show "A Prairie Home Companion": *Bible study can get you out of bed in the morning to do what you need and want to do.* Bible study groups can be filled with laughter, questions, insights, and a deepening awareness of God's presence and leading. Bible study can build community and empower mission. But for that to happen, you need to engage the world within the New Testament. I pray that *Reading the New Testament for the First Time* will help you do so.

QUESTIONS FOR DISCUSSION

1. In two minutes, write down the words or phrases that come to you when you hear the words "New Testament." These words could be ideas, images, feelings, anything. Just let them pop out of your mind and onto the paper. Do not try to evaluate them as good or not.

2. When you have finished this exercise, look over your responses. What do they tell you about your perspectives and feelings toward the New Testament?

3. Now, more deliberately, think about how you have encountered the New Testament (or the Bible more generally) up to this point in your life. What do you remember about those encounters?

4. As you begin this book, what are some of your main questions about the New Testament? What would you like to know? What do you most hope to walk away with as a result of this short study?

CHAPTER 1

What Will I Find
When I Open the Bible?

Basic Facts

Imagine that you buy a new electronic device that requires assembly at home. When you open the box, a page falls out that lists all the parts needed to put the device together. This chapter is similar to that list. It describes what you need to know about the basic parts of the New Testament for it to make sense when you pick it up.

We begin with two very basic questions: How does one get a copy of the New Testament? and what does it mean to speak of the "Holy Bible"? I will introduce you to the parts of the Bible (books, chapters, verses) and help you understand what is meant by the term "New Testament." Then we will examine more closely what exactly the New Testament is and how you can learn to find various passages. Following a review of how we received the New Testament, I conclude with a plea for you to carry your New Testament with you.

Where Can I Get a Copy of the New Testament?

The first question facing a person who wants to explore the New Testament is simply: "Where can I get a copy?" You can acquire a copy in one of two ways. (1) Perhaps the easier way is to locate a copy of the whole Bible. The Bible is one volume made up of two parts, with the Old Testament part making up the first three-quarters of the Bible and the New Testament part making up the last quarter. (2) The other way is to locate a copy of the New Testament by itself. You can pick up a copy of the Bible or the New Testament in many bookstores; you can order a copy from an online bookseller, or even begin by checking out a copy from a library. Almost every church would be thrilled to give you a copy of the New Testament. The place of the New Testament in the Bible is discussed more fully below.

For many years the New Testament and the Bible were known mainly by those titles. However, in the last forty years these books have sometimes been published under new titles as a way of making them appear more contemporary and inviting. The following are some recent fresh titles given to the Bible: *Good News Bible, The Living Bible, The Message,* and *God's Word.* These are all new translations of the Bible.[1]

What Does the Phrase "Holy Bible" Mean?

As I have already noted, the New Testament is part of a larger book called the Bible or the Holy Bible. The English word "Bible" comes from the Greek word *biblios,* which simply means "book." The word "bibliography" comes from the same Greek word. The Greek word for "bible" does not have a special religious meaning but can refer to any book. The word "holy" in this context means to be set apart by God for a special purpose. The people who gave this book the name "Holy Bible" believed that this literature could be of special use in helping people recognize and respond to God's presence and purposes.[2]

1. The New Testament was originally written in the Greek language. Scholars must translate it from Greek into English. Because words and phrases in Greek can often be translated into English in more than one way, there are many different translations. Several popular ones are discussed in Appendix A (pp. 179-81).

2. As implied in the Introduction, Christians and others have different interpretations of just how God works through this revealing process. These options are discussed more fully in Chapter 13 (pp. 167-78).

The Parts of the Bible: Small and Large

When you are looking for a passage in the Bible, it is important to know something about the basic layout. The Bible, you will find, is divided into small parts (books, chapters, and verses) and large parts (the Old and New Testaments).

The Small Parts of the Bible: Books, Chapters, and Verses

The Bible is made up of smaller divisions or books. The books are not long. In fact, if each biblical book were published as a separate volume, each would really be more like a booklet, and some would barely be leaflets.

Each *book* has a title. When you open the Bible, you can tell which book of the Bible you are reading by looking at the top of the page. There you will see a name, such as Genesis, Proverbs, Isaiah, Matthew, Romans, James, or Revelation.

The titles for these books come from different sources. Most of them derive from the contents of the book, or from the name of the author, or from the city in which the intended audience for the book lived. For example, the name Matthew (the title of the first Gospel) came about because some early Christians thought that a person named Matthew wrote it. The book of Romans was directed to the group of Christians in the city of Rome.

Each book is also divided into *chapters* and *verses*.[3] The chapters are not long; most of them would take up only one single-spaced page. They are numbered in sequence, with the number of the chapter printed in large type at its beginning. The longest book in the New Testament — the book of Acts — has only 28 chapters. The shortest books are only one chapter (for example, Philemon).

The verses are short segments within each chapter. Each verse is numbered, with the number usually appearing as a superscript or in parentheses at the beginning of a verse. Many verses are about a

---

3. Some newer versions of the New Testament include chapters but not verses.

sentence in length; some are shorter, and occasionally some are longer. You can see an example of chapter and verse numbering in Box 1.

Box 1. Example of Chapters and Verses

13 ¹If I speak in the tongues of mortals and of angels, but do not have love, I am a noisy gong or a clanging cymbal. ²And if I have prophetic powers and understand all mysteries and all knowledge, and if I have all faith, so as to remove mountains, but do not have love, I am nothing. ³If I give away all my possessions, and if I hand over my body so that I may boast, but do not have love, I gain nothing.

This example comes from the book of 1 Corinthians. The bold number 13 is the chapter number. The superscript numbers 1, 2, and 3 are the verse numbers. In a worship bulletin, Bible study guide, or other resource, the reference would be 1 Corinthians 13:1-3. This expression would be spoken as "First Corinthians thirteen, verses one to three" or, more simply, as "First Corinthians thirteen, one to three."

A passage is referred to by chapter and verse number. When writing a passage, you write the name of the book, followed by a space, then the chapter number, followed immediately by a colon, with the verses immediately following. The verses are indicated from the first to the last with a hyphen in between:

book name (space) chapter number:verse-verse
For example: John 1:1-5

This designation refers to the book of John, chapter 1, verses 1 through 5. When saying aloud a Bible reference, you give the name of the book, then the chapter number, then the verse numbers. For example, John 1:1-5 is "John one, verses one through five," or, more simply, "John one, one through five."

A passage sometimes cuts across chapter boundaries, as in:

1 Thessalonians 4:13–5:11.

This designation refers to the book of 1 Thessalonians, chapter 4, verse 13 through chapter 5, verse 11. Aloud, it would sound like this: "First Thessalonians four, verse thirteen through five, verse eleven," or "First Thessalonians four, thirteen through five, eleven."

Four books in the New Testament are only one chapter in length: Philemon, Jude, and 2 and 3 John. These books do not have chapter numbers. We cite these little books only by book title and verse numbers, as in:

Jude 5-7.

When referencing this passage aloud, you would say, "Jude, verses 5 through 7," or simply "Jude five through seven."

The Large Parts of the Bible: Old and New Testaments

All Christians agree that the Bible contains two main sections — the Old Testament and the New Testament. All churches agree that the New Testament contains the 27 books that are found in any Bible. They are the complete New Testament.

However, some churches include different books in their lists of books in the Old Testament. I mention the different lists of books of the Old Testament so you will have a sense of what you are seeing when you thumb your way toward the New Testament.

Most Protestants use a Bible that contains a total of 66 books — 39 in the Old Testament and 27 in the New Testament.[4] I should

---

4. The Protestant movement originated in the sixteenth century to protest certain aspects of Roman Catholic practice. Today, few Protestant churches actually protest the Roman Catholic Church. Indeed, most Protestant churches enjoy friendly relationships with Roman Catholics. We continue to use the designation "Protestant" as a matter of convenience.

be upfront and say that this position is the one I hold. The Roman Catholic Church uses a Bible that has an additional number of books, and the Orthodox Churches use a Bible that has even more. The books of the Old Testament are listed in Box 2. The books of the

Box 2. Basic 39 Books of the Old Testament

Genesis	2 Chronicles	Daniel
Exodus	Ezra	Hosea
Leviticus	Nehemiah	Joel
Numbers	Esther	Amos
Deuteronomy	Job	Obadiah
Joshua	Psalms	Jonah
Judges	Proverbs	Micah
Ruth	Ecclesiastes	Nahum
1 Samuel	Song of Solomon	Habakkuk
2 Samuel	Isaiah	Zephaniah
1 Kings	Jeremiah	Haggai
2 Kings	Lamentations	Zechariah
1 Chronicles	Ezekiel	Malachi

Additional Books in the Roman Catholic Old Testament

Tobit	Ecclesiasticus (also	Daniel (Prayer of
Judith	known as Sirach or	Azariah, Susanna, Bel
Additions to Esther	Ben Sira)	and the Dragon)
Wisdom of Solomon	Baruch	1 and 2 Maccabees
(sometimes known	Letter of Jeremiah	(pronounced
simply as Wisdom)	Additions to the Book of	"MACK-a-bees").

Additional Books in the Orthodox Old Testament

1 Esdras (also known as	is included in an ap-	3 Esdras
3 Ezra)	pendix but is not con-	Odes, including the
3 Maccabees	sidered canonical)	Prayer of Manasseh
4 Maccabees (this book	2 Esdras	Psalms of Solomon

Additional Books Adopted by the Ethiopian Orthodox Church

Enoch	2 Esdras (also known as
Jubilees	4 Ezra)

New Testament are given below. The Old Testament is in the first part of the Bible, with the New Testament following in the latter part of the Bible. The contents of the Old Testament are summarized in Chapter 3.

What Is in the New Testament?

The New Testament contains 27 books (see Box 3). These books can be classified as five basic kinds of literature. I mention these classifications because they will help you know what kind of literature to expect when you look into one of these books.

Box 3. The Books of the New Testament in Order

Matthew	Ephesians	1 Peter
Mark	Philippians	2 Peter
Luke	Colossians	1 John
John	1 Thessalonians	2 John
Acts (sometimes known	2 Thessalonians	3 John
as the Acts of the	1 Timothy	Jude
Apostles)	2 Timothy	Revelation (note: the
Romans	Titus	word Revelation is sin-
1 Corinthians	Philemon	gular, not the plural
2 Corinthians	Hebrews	"Revelations")
Galatians	James	

---

1. The *Gospels* tell the story of Jesus, each from a different perspective.[5] The Gospels are Matthew, Mark, Luke, and John. These books, found at the very beginning of the New Testament, are narratives that contain events, sayings, and extended speeches.

2. Many scholars think the book of Acts is a work of *history*. Acts is a narrative that tells of Jesus' closest followers after his resurrec-

---

5. The word "gospel" translates a Greek word meaning "good news." The Gospels contain the good news about Jesus.

tion and departure for heaven.[6] The first part of Acts focuses on the church in Jerusalem, while the latter sections tell the story of Paul. The book of Acts was written by someone named Luke, who also wrote the Gospel of Luke. From my point of view, the book of Acts is not a separate category of literature (such as history) but continues the story of the Gospel of Luke.

3. The *letters* constitute 17 books of the New Testament. The letters were written by leaders in the church to specific congregations (or groups of congregations) to help them deal with questions that had come up. Some scholars divide the letters into three sub-categories:

> Letters certainly written by Paul: Romans, 1 and 2 Corinthians, Galatians, Philippians, 1 Thessalonians, Philemon.
> Letters written by some of Paul's followers: Colossians, Ephesians, 2 Thessalonians, 1 and 2 Timothy, Titus.
> Letters written by other writers: James, 1 and 2 Peter, 1, 2, and 3 John, Jude.

4. Along with many scholars, I believe the book of *Hebrews* is an early Christian *sermon.* A few interpreters consider Hebrews to be a letter, but it seems to possess more of the characteristics of an ancient sermon.

5. The book of Revelation is literature that describes what the end of time will look like. This kind of literature doesn't have a modern equivalent and is called an apocalypse — pronounced "ah-POCK-ah-lips." The book of Revelation — like other writings of this kind in the ancient world — used word-pictures to interpret the present and to encourage people to live in hope as they anticipated God's future redemptive activity.

---

6. This is sometimes called the ascension because Jesus floated or ascended into the heavens.

> **Box 4. A Little Practical Advice for Finding a Passage**
>
> Sometimes you might be in a service of worship or a Bible study group or some other setting where you need to locate a passage quickly. If you are not sure where that book is located in the New Testament, I suggest that you look immediately at the Table of Contents in the front of the Bible. Otherwise, you may spend several minutes flipping through the New Testament, and the preacher or the group may have moved on before you have even found the passage.

How We Got the New Testament

This story of how we got the New Testament has two phases: (1) how the individual books of the New Testament came to be written, and (2) how they came to be regarded as sacred.

How the Individual Books of the New Testament Came to Be Written

The first phase began with Jesus, who lived about 4 B.C.E. through 30 C.E. As far as we know, no one wrote anything about him during that time.[7] However, soon after his resurrection, Jesus' followers began to tell stories about him and to spread his message.

---

7. We discuss the dates of Jesus' life (4 B.C.E. to 30 C.E.) in Chapter 3. The letters B.C.E. and C.E. are relatively new abbreviations for "Before the Common Era" (B.C.E.) and "Common Era" (C.E.). They refer to the years that are common to both Judaism and Christianity (C.E.) and the years before that time (B.C.E.). The birth of Jesus signals the beginning of the Common Era. A growing number of Christians prefer these expressions to the more familiar "A.D." and "B.C." "A.D." came from *anno Domini*, Latin for "in the year of our Lord," and "B.C." means "Before Christ." The language B.C.E. and C.E. is more respectful of Judaism than A.D. and B.C. On Christian negativity toward Judaism, see pp. 34-35.

The first book of the New Testament to be written was 1 Thessalonians. A man named Paul wrote it around 49-51 C.E. in response to issues in the congregation in the city of Thessalonica.[8] Paul wrote six additional letters over the next ten or twelve years.

In 70 C.E., the Romans destroyed the temple in Jerusalem in reaction to a Jewish uprising. Jesus' followers had collected and continued to tell stories about him, but they had not developed a narrative of his life. At around 70 C.E. Mark became the first to do so. Matthew and Luke came next (80-90 C.E.), with John writing last (90-100 C.E.). At the same time that the Gospel writers were at work, other authors wrote other documents — letters, a sermon (Hebrews), and an extended vision of the end time (the book of Revelation). The last books in our New Testament to be written — 1, 2, and 3 John — were penned about 100 to 110.

Soon after his resurrection, Jesus' followers began to tell stories about him and to spread his message.

*How the Books of the New Testament
Came to Be Regarded as Sacred*

The second phase lasted from about 100 C.E. to 367 C.E. The church faced the question, "Which books generated by followers of Jesus should we regard as trustworthy and having authority?" This question was complicated by the fact that many other books were written about the same time or shortly after the books in the New Testament and yet these were not included in our New Testament. Some early churches read these books, such as the Gospel of the Ebionites, the Gospel of Mary, the Gospel of Thomas, the Acts of Paul and Thecla, the Shepherd of Hermas, the Epistle of Barnabas, and the Teaching of the Twelve Apostles. Some of these books pre-

---

8. Scholars cannot always be sure of the dates when documents were written. In such cases, they indicate possible dates of composition by giving a range of likely possibilities, such as 49-51 or 80-90.

sent a different kind of Jesus, while others tell stories of Jesus' closest and earliest followers.

From 100 to 367 C.E., many of the churches drifted toward honoring the 27 books that we recognize as the New Testament. Yet questions persisted as to whether some of these actually belonged in an official church collection. Books such as 2 and 3 John, 2 Peter, Jude, James, and the book of Revelation all faced such questions.

In 367 a pivotal moment occurred when a bishop, a leader in the early church, named Athanasius ("ath-uh-NAY-she-us") wrote a letter to the churches of that time that for the first time listed the 27 books that we know as the New Testament as the church's official Scriptures. Following the bishop's letter, most of the churches came to agree on the New Testament as we now have it.

Why did the church settle on these 27 books? Many of the books not included present troubling views. Some of those not included described our material world — matter itself — as evil. Others portrayed the God of the Old Testament as a different, wrathful deity from the loving God of the New Testament. Still others did not present Jesus as an actual flesh-and-blood human being (he only appeared to be); the goal of life, according to these books, was to escape from the material world into the nonmaterial heaven. Some of their writers believed that their personal visions had more authority regarding what to believe than did the early Christian tradition reflected in the books that made up the New Testament. The church concluded that such writings misrepresented God's purposes.

Over time, the church recognized the 27 books in our present New Testament on the basis of three informal criteria. (a) The church believed that the content of the 27 books was in harmony with the earliest Christian tradition. (b) The books were widely accepted by the churches (and not just by small groups or sects). (c) The church considered the 27 books to be more ancient than the other books. People in antiquity valued old things, so the older the books were thought to be, the more impressive they would seem.

Ancient Technology and the New Testament

In those days, people usually wrote on papyrus ("pa-PIE-russ"), a paperlike substance made by splitting reeds and mashing them together. People sometimes wrote on animal skins that had been tanned and made flexible. We do not have any of the original papyri (the plural of papyrus) or animal skins, but we do have thousands of copies. The earliest is a fragment of the Gospel of John about the

Luke 24:51-53 and John 1:1-16 from an early manuscript of the New Testament, around 175-225 C.E.

Pap.Bodmer.XIV-XV (P75), p.2A 8r.

© Biblioteca Apostolica Vaticana.

size of a postage stamp dating from 115 C.E. Since there were no printing presses until the 1400s, these copies were made by hand.

The scribes who copied the manuscripts sometimes made changes in the wording. Some of these changes were accidental, as when my mind gets ahead of my fingers and I mis-type a word. But some of the changes were intentional; the copyist thought that the manuscript needed clarification or change. For example, the most reliable copies of the early manuscripts of the Gospel of Mark end at 16:8 with the story of an empty tomb but no appearance of the resurrected Jesus. Scribes added Mark 16:9-20 so that the text of the Gospel of Mark would end with an appearance of the resurrected Jesus. In the added material, Jesus says, "These signs will accompany those who believe: . . . they will pick up snakes in their hands; and if they drink any deadly thing, it will not hurt them" (Mark 16:17-18). The notions of safely picking up snakes and drinking poison are not elsewhere found in standard Christian literature in the first century. Since this is so foreign and not in the best copies of the manuscripts, these verses are considered to be a less-than-likely part of the original composition of the Gospel of Mark.

The chapter and verse numbers we discussed earlier were not in the original copies of the Bible. They were added in the late Middle Ages. Most of the chapters and verses divide the biblical material into meaningful units, but some chapters and verses are divided at strange points. As you learn to be a careful reader of the New Testament, you will learn not to limit your reading to chapters and verses but look for the larger literary context of a section of the New Testament. In that way you will be reading it the same way that someone who had a copy made of ancient parchment or animal hide would have.

Take Your New Testament with You

Carpenters bring their tools to the job site. Similarly, Christians should carry the New Testament to worship and study. The Bible is a basic tool. You can follow along while the Bible is read aloud in worship or while a group is pondering a passage in Bible study. There is no substitute for reading the words of the Bible with your own eyes.

The text itself can raise questions, spark insights, and open up worlds that you could not imagine on your own. While many congregations provide pew Bibles,

Carpenters bring their tools to the job site. Similarly, Christians should carry the New Testament to worship and study.

having your own copy allows you to make notes. Over time, your own copy of the Bible may begin to feel like a trusty friend.

QUESTIONS FOR DISCUSSION

1. Name three things from this chapter that were new discoveries for you. How do you think they will help you navigate the New Testament (and the larger Bible?)

2. Now for an exercise whose object is to practice finding passages. If you are in a group, you might have races to see who can find these passages the fastest.

> Matthew 5:1-12 (the Beatitudes — a series of blessings that open a sermon by Jesus referred to as the Sermon on the Mount)
>
> Acts 9:1-19 (the call of Paul)
>
> Romans 8:26-27 (the Spirit helps us)
>
> 1 Peter 4:7-11 (prepare for the end)
>
> 2 John 4-6 (John addresses the "dear lady")
>
> Revelation 4:1-11 (a word picture of heaven)

3. It is helpful to have the order of the New Testament books memorized if you want to be proficient in finding passages in them. I challenge you to learn the books of the New Testament in order. If memorizing is a challenge, you might make up a song or create memory devices to help you remember.

CHAPTER 2

The World of the New Testament

As I write this book, my spouse and I have two children in college. When each child was born, we opened a college fund for that child in the stock market and we made monthly contributions. The morning that I began this chapter (in the summer of 2009), I needed to withdraw some money from the stock funds to pay our children's tuition. When I looked at how much money was in the funds, the balances were 30 percent smaller than they were the year before. I was shocked. I felt betrayed and angry. Fortunately, I made this discovery when I was alone. Otherwise I might have offended other people with the strength of my reaction. I spoke in unflattering ways (and with considerable heat) about certain individuals, corporations, and government leaders.

To understand what happened to our stock funds — and my response — it might help you to know our stockbroker and our habits of spending and saving. Being aware of my personality might help you understand why I reacted in a lamentable way. But you would need to be aware of more than our personal affairs. You would also need to know that the economy of the United States went into a recession in the fall of 2008 and had not recovered as of the time I wrote this chapter. By the time I saw the balance in our shrinking stock funds, our nation knew what values and people had caused the recession. It is no small wonder that I spoke of those people in an uncomplimentary way. To understand my unpleasant reaction, you would need to understand the larger forces at work in our economic life.

Similarly, the world in which the New Testament writers lived was made up of two related elements whose interaction is important in understanding the mind-set of the writers of the New Testament. (1) The New Testament was written by Jewish people. They wrote from the perspective of the Old Testament and Jewish history. (2) The Roman Empire ruled the entire Mediterranean basin during the writing of the New Testament, including the land of Judea (the land where the Jewish people lived). The presence and behavior of Rome affected the New Testament writers.

A Little History of the Jewish People

As noted above, the central characters in the New Testament are Jewish.[1] Many of the first readers of the New Testament were Jewish. The first time they read the books that became the New Testament, they viewed those books as extending the Old Testament story. Consequently, when reading the New Testament we benefit from a basic outline of the story of the Jewish people.

> **Many of the first readers of the New Testament were Jewish. The first time they read the books that became the New Testament, they viewed those books as extending the Old Testament story.**

---

1. The names "Jew" and "Jewish" were used extensively at the time of the New Testament and have been since. They derive from the names Judah and Judea. The former was the name of one of the twelve tribes of Israel and of the southern nation when Israel divided into two nations (Israel in the north and Judah in the south). At the time of the New Testament, the area around Jerusalem was often known as Judea. Throughout much of the Old Testament period, the Jewish people were often called the children (or people) of Israel. That language was still occasionally used at the time of the New Testament. For Judea see the maps on pp. 27 and 29.

The Creation of the World, Life in Paradise, and the Fall

The first two chapters of the Bible describe God creating the world (Genesis 1:1–2:24). In Genesis 1, God created the world by speaking it into existence: "And God said, 'Let there be light,' and there was light." Genesis 2:4-24 is a second story of creation; it highlights God creating the first human being out of the dust of the earth and the second human being from a rib taken from the first. This first couple, Adam and Eve, lived in the Garden of Eden (the name "Eden" means "delight" in Hebrew) in perfect community with one another, with animals, and with nature. The relationship of the couple was one of equals, and they lived in nearly complete freedom. However, God did forbid them to eat the fruit of a particular tree, the tree of the knowledge of good and evil.

In Genesis 3, a snake tempted Eve and Adam to disobey this one rule and eat a piece of fruit from the forbidden tree, telling them that doing so would make them "like God." After they ate the fruit, God cursed the world. God punished the snake by making it crawl. The curse led to a rift between humankind and the world of animals and ecosystems. Further consequences were that the woman would suffer pain in child-bearing and that the early equality would be replaced with her subjection to the man. Work became a burden and survival became difficult. Christians often refer to this event as "the fall" (that is, the fall from life in Eden). Existence continued after the fall, but not as God originally planned.

The Beginnings of the People Israel (the Jewish People)

In Genesis 4–11, God tried to help the human family make its way through the fallen world. When that failed, God decided to work with one human community as a model for all others. According to Genesis 12:1-3, God chose Sarah and Abraham for a special mission. God would bless them so that their children would become a thriving people, and that people would show the other peoples in the world how to receive God's blessing. This is what it means to be "the chosen people": to be chosen by God to model God's ways for all peoples of the world. Scholars date the stories about the patriarch Abraham at around 1800 B.C.E. These ancient stories mark the beginning of the Jewish people as a distinct group.

> This is what it means to be "the chosen people": to be chosen by God to model God's ways for all peoples of the world.

We need to introduce a word that is very important to the New Testament: gentiles. The Jewish people came to divide the human family into two groups: the Jewish people who live out of the tradition of Sarah and Abraham, and the gentiles, all the other peoples of the world, who often worshiped idols and violated God's purposes. Everyone who is not Jewish is gentile. God designated the Jewish people as a light or to guide and teach the gentiles.

From Sarah and Abraham to Jesus

We can summarize the history of the Jewish community in a few paragraphs. When God called Sarah and Abraham to be a blessing, God promised to be their God and to go with them. God made this promise as an act of grace, that is, as an act of unmerited favor. Sarah and Abraham did not do anything to earn God's love and blessing. Such a promise is called a covenant. A covenant is based on a promise that one party makes to another. Covenants in the Bible include principles that guide people in how to live in a way that is pleasing to God and that will bring a blessing. Sarah and Abraham had one son, Isaac, whose descendants grew to a sufficiently large number eventually to form twelve tribes. They came to be called the children of Israel, named after one of Sarah and Abraham's grandsons. The name Israel means "one who struggles with God." That name is a clue to the nature of this people: they struggle with God.

When a famine left them without food, the descendants of Sarah and Abraham traveled to Egypt to purchase food supplies. While they did get food, they were eventually enslaved in Egypt. God freed them from slavery through an event called the Exodus, one of the most important stories in the Old Testament. During the Exodus, God gave them the Ten Commandments at Mount Sinai (pronounced "SIGH-nigh," with a long "i" in each syllable). In addition to the Ten Commandments, they received more than 600 additional commandments or principles. Among other things, these principles directed the people to eat certain foods and to avoid others. In time these rules led to what Jews today call "kosher" rules. Another aspect of the early Jewish community's life was the care it was to show for widows, orphans, strangers, and the poor. Important as well was the rule that all males were to be circumcised. The purpose of circumcision and keeping the food laws, as well as the concern over justice, was to remind Sarah and Abraham and their descendants that they were in covenant with God and had to live in ways that demonstrated God's purposes.

After the people of Israel were liberated from Egypt, they conquered the land of Canaan (located in about the same place as the present state of Israel; see the map on p. 27), where they lived in a loose confederacy and were governed by leaders the Bible refers to as judges. These weren't judges in the way we think of them today, but more like leaders of a tribal militia responsible for the protection of the confederacy of Israelite clans. They also sought to keep the burgeoning nation focused on its holy laws. Growing dissatisfied with this loose arrangement, the heirs of Sarah and Abraham wanted to be like the other nations of the world and so asked God for a king. Saul was their first king, soon followed by David, the most famous ancient Israelite king. Solomon ruled after David.

Following Solomon's reign the one nation was divided into two: the northern nation called Israel and the southern nation called Judah. During this time, the people turned away from God, worshiped idols, and exploited the poor. Through prophets such as Amos, Isaiah, and Jeremiah, God condemned their behavior and allowed the Babylonians (who lived in present-day Iraq) to conquer them, destroy the temple, and take their leaders into exile. The exiles remained in Babylon for two generations.

The children of Israel were freed from exile when the Persians defeated Babylon. The Persians allowed the people to return to their homeland, where they rebuilt the temple and lived under colonial rule, first of Persia, then of various other governments. The Romans began to rule the land of Israel in 63 B.C.E. During these years, Jewish people continued to struggle with how to be faithful to God.

Jewish Life between the Testaments

The most important phenomenon outside of Judaism to take place in the ancient world between the return from exile and the beginning of Roman rule in Palestine was the conquest and rule of Alexander the Great (356-323 B.C.E.). He brought much of the Mediterranean world under one government and instituted the policy of Hellenization. The word "Hellenization" reveals the nature of this policy, for it comes from a Greek word that simply means "Greek." Hellenization was Alexander's attempt to establish Greek culture throughout the Mediterranean basin, so we might refer to this policy as Grecization. Although Alexander died at age 33 and thus personally ruled only a short time, Hellenization continued for three hundred years.

Hellenization is important for Judaism and for the New Testament for two reasons. First, it brought Greek gods, Greek people, Greek institutions, and Greek culture into villages, cities, and nations all around the Mediterranean basin. The Jewish people — like other groups — had to answer the question, How do we respond to Hellenization?

- Do we embrace it?
- Do we reject it?
- Do we find some middle ground whereby we learn to live with it but do not fully embrace it?

These questions were especially important to the Jewish community, who had one God whom they believed to be universally sovereign. They saw themselves as a separate community whose purpose was to witness to God's ways, to bless all peoples, and live out a distinct culture and practices (such as avoiding idolatry, practicing circumcision, honoring their own dietary practices, and living in covenant). The Roman government adapted the policies of Hellenization toward Roman gods and culture and pressed them even further. Jewish groups responded to Hellenization and Romanization in all of the ways just mentioned (see "The Jewish People at the Time of the New Testament," pp. 28-31 below).

Second, Hellenization made it possible for people from different parts of the world to have much more contact with one another than previously. Alexander and his successors established a simplified form of the Greek language (called Koine — pronounced "KOY-nay" — which means "shared") throughout the Mediterranean. Everyone could speak the same language. The Romans built roads and established shipping to enable people and goods to get from one place to another. Letter writing became commonplace. For the first time in Mediterranean history, people could move from one area to another with relative ease. By the time of the New Testament, more Jewish people lived outside the Holy Land than in it. This migration is called the Diaspora — pronounced "die-AS-por-uh" — which means "dispersion." In many parts of the Mediterranean world, people could leave one religion and join another; prior to this time, a person was born into the religion of her or his geographic area and pretty much remained in that religion for life. However, in the Hellenistic age, conversion from one religion to another began to take place. These developments in communication, social order, and religion made it possible for the message of the Jesus movement to spread throughout the Mediterranean world in a way that would have been impossible at the beginning of the Hellenistic age.

At the outset of the Hellenistic period, all the books of the Old Testament were written except one, Daniel, which was written about 168-165 B.C.E. However, the Jewish people wrote many other books, mostly to help the Jewish community respond to the pressures of Hellenization. This material is sometimes called the Intertestamental literature since it was written between the Old and New Testaments. These books fall into two large groups.

One group of books that is included in the Roman Catholic and Orthodox canons (or lists of books in their Bibles) but not in the Jewish or Protestant canons is often called the Apocrypha of the Old Testament or the apocryphal/deuterocanonical books of the Old Testament. Some Bibles today insert these books between the Old Testament and the New Testament. These writings encourage their readers to believe that they can make their way faithfully through the world of Hellenization without fully embracing Hellenization, thus remaining wary of compromising their faith and practice. These books warn readers against threats to Jewish life and urge faithfulness. Several of these writings make some use of Greek philosophy in how they express their ideas.

Among the most-well-known apocryphal writings are 1 and 2 Maccabees, which tell the story of a successful Jewish revolt led by the Maccabees family against one of the foreign rulers of the Holy Land about 168-165 B.C.E. Other well-known writings include the Wisdom of Solomon — a philosophical tract which adapts Plato's idea that the soul is immortal to Jewish thought. A book that goes by three names — Ecclesiasticus, Sirach, or the Wisdom of Jesus Son of Sirach (this Jesus is earlier than the New Testament Jesus) — is a compendium of sayings on how to live faithfully. Still other apocryphal writings include Tobit, Judith, Esther (with additions), Baruch, Letter of Jeremiah, Prayer of Azariah, Susanna, Bel and the Dragon, Prayer of Manasseh, Psalm 151, 1, 2, and 3 Esdras, and 3 and 4 Maccabees. 4 Maccabees makes extensive use of Greek philosophy.

Another body of literature is not included in the Protestant or Catholic canons but provides the basic theological framework for the writings of Paul, Matthew, Mark, Luke-Acts, and several other books in the New Testament. This large body of material is made up largely of prophecies about the end of time. It is often called apocalyptic literature. People new to Bible study sometimes confuse the names Apocrypha and apocalyptic. Another name for this end-of-time literature is Pseudepigrapha (pronounced "soo-deh-PIG-ra-fa"), an expression which literally but misleadingly means "false writing." These materials, though written in the Hellenistic age, present themselves as having been written by famous people long, long before. They bear names of heroes of old, such as Enoch, Baruch, and the Testaments of the Twelve Patriarchs. These books tend to reject Hellenization. You will find the apocalyptic part of the book 2 Esdras (sometimes called 4 Ezra) in the Apocrypha.

This end-time literature teaches that history is divided into two ages — the present evil age (with its Hellenizing phenomena) that is soon to pass away, and the coming new world in which all things will take place according to God's purposes. The apocalyptic writers believed that the present world is under the heel of repressive forces — such as Satan, the demons, and governments ruling through violence — that are so powerful that they must be completely destroyed before a new world can emerge. Hellenization was perceived by the authors of this end-time literature as a prime example of the problems of the old, evil world that had to pass away because Hellenization could so easily lead Jewish people into compromising their faith.

The new world is often called the Realm of God (the kingdom of God), the new creation, or the age to come. The old age was to give way to the new through an apocalypse — a moment when God will come with the angels from heaven to destroy the old, evil world and establish the new age of his Realm. The Greek word "apocalyptic" means "to reveal." This literature reveals to readers what the writers believed was the proper interpretation of history so that the Jewish community would be prepared for the end of the old and the beginning of the new. The purpose of this literature is to offer people hope in the new age so that they can endure the difficulties of the present.

The apocalyptic writers express themselves in visions or word-pictures, often of fantastic beasts, amazing voyages, and dramatic images. While such language is sometimes hard for people today to understand, people in the ancient world could read it as easily as we can read cartoons in the newspaper. The book of Revelation in the New Testament is an example of an apocalyptic writing.

Life in the Roman Empire

The Romans began to rule the land of Israel in 63 B.C.E. During these years, the Jewish people continued to struggle with how to be faithful to God. The New Testament writers joined this struggle.

The New Testament writers all lived in the Roman Empire. This empire included all the nations on the edge of the Mediterranean Sea as well as parts of Europe (including parts of England). The empire was roughly the same size as the United States today (see map on p. 27).

The Roman Empire was controlled by an emperor (called Caesar) in conjunction with the Roman Senate. The empire enforced its will through a large army with divisions garrisoned throughout the empire. In addition, the army was often engaged in fighting on the borders of the empire. Life in the empire was thus permeated by violence and by the anxiety that accompanies violence and the threat of violence.

In the year 44 B.C.E., just before the time of the New Testament, the Roman Senate voted to give the deceased Julius Caesar "divine honors." The Roman government thus elevated a human being to a status approaching that of the Roman gods. Over the course of the New Testament period, leaders of the Roman Empire increasingly regarded the emperor as such a figure. Roman citizens sometimes referred to Caesar as the "son of God." An imperial cult grew up around the emperor.

The social organization of the Roman Empire was a rigid class hierarchy. At the top were a small number of people from the upper classes who presided over a patronage system. This meant that people in the lower ranks of society were expected to honor the upper class when they met them in the street or when they approached the wealthy for a personal audience. This honor would be repaid by favors, and thus merchants could become affluent. People who owned their own land had a higher social status than the landless day laborers. Slaves, of course, were at the bottom of the heap.

One percent of the population of the empire owned half the land. The empire had a small number of people equivalent to to-

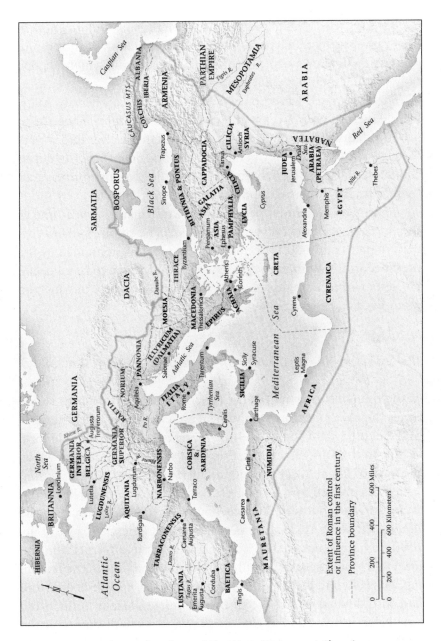

The Roman Empire at the Time of the New Testament Showing a
Numbers of Cities Important to the New Testament Story

day's middle class (often merchants), with the vast majority of people in poverty. As much as a third of the population of the empire was enslaved. Many people lived from day to day and had little hope of improving their personal circumstances.

The Roman government taxed the population heavily. Many people owed money. To pay their debts people often made themselves indentured servants, that is, they sold themselves into slavery for a few years. In addition, people who had no debts but also had no capital could indenture themselves in order to raise money and thereby improve their economic situations.

The New Testament period is sometimes known as a time of the *Pax Romana,* Latin for "peace of Rome." The empire had few civil disturbances during this period, but the quiet was enforced by the presence of the Roman sword. The peace of Rome masked social tensions within Roman society as well as the poverty in which so many lived.

The Jewish People in Judea at the Time of the New Testament

At the time of the writing of the New Testament, Judea was sometimes the name for the geographical area approximating the state of Israel today and sometimes the name for the area outside Jerusalem. In the Old Testament, that area was sometimes known as the land of Israel. After the monarchy (Saul, David, and Solomon) Israel was divided into two states; the northern one was known as Israel and the southern one was known as Judah. In 135 C.E., the Roman Emperor Hadrian renamed the area Palestine, a word derived from the name of the Phoenicians, enemies of Israel who had lived in the land several centuries before. At the time of the renaming, Hadrian had just put down a revolt of the Jewish people and had forbidden them to live in or around Jerusalem. Calling the area Palestine was one of Hadrian's strategies to disempower the Jewish people. The map on page 29 shows Judea and surrounding areas at the time of Jesus.

During the Roman occupation, life in Judea resembled life in

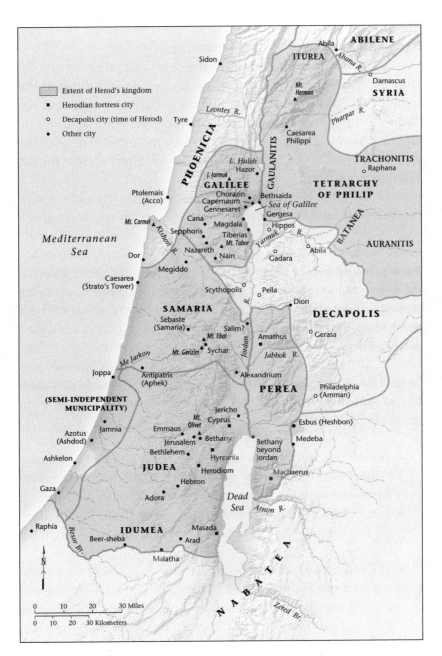

Judea and Surrounding Territories at the Time of Jesus. The Romans Sometimes Referred to This Whole Area as "Judea."

the broader Roman Empire: military presence, social hierarchy, heavy taxes, poverty, anxiety, and bitterness.

The Romans employed Herod the Great and others to rule the Holy Land on their behalf. Many Jewish people worshiped at the temple in Jerusalem, and many gathered every Friday night and Saturday morning in synagogues for local worship, instruction, and socializing. Jewish males were circumcised, a mark that reminded the Jewish people that they belonged to the God of Israel and not the Roman gods or Caesar.

In Judea, most Jewish people lived in small communities and in rural areas. Jerusalem was by far the largest city. Most of them spoke Aramaic (a dialect of Hebrew) in everyday life. Many also spoke Greek.

During the Roman occupation, life in Judea resembled life in the Roman Empire: military presence, social hierarchy, heavy taxes, poverty, anxiety, and bitterness.

Throughout the occupations of their land — from the Persians to the Romans — a central question with which the Jewish people struggled was: "How should we live in relationship to the occupying power so as to be faithful to our mission?" Different groups responded to this question in quite different ways. Jesus and his followers faced the same question.

- The Sadducees (pronounced "SAD-you-sees") along with many priests were the Jewish upper class. They cooperated with Rome and benefited economically from this cooperation.
- The Zealots bitterly opposed Rome and expected God to liberate Israel by means of a holy war in which they would fight for God.
- The Pharisees (pronounced "FAIR-uh-sees") sought a middle way between the Sadducees and the Zealots. A lay-led renewal movement, they believed that the essence of Judaism consisted of following the law in one's personal and home life. They sought to cooperate with Rome just enough to avoid being harassed but otherwise kept their distance from Rome.
- Those groups that had hopes that they were living in the end of

time (this way of looking at the world is sometimes called apocalyptic) believed that God was about to end the present age (which would include the destruction of the Roman Empire) and that people should prepare for the new age by repenting (including repenting of collusion with Rome) and await the new world. As I will explain more fully in the next chapter, I see Jesus and his followers as such a group.

- The common people, whom some ancient Jewish writers referred to as "the people of the land," represented the large number of Jewish people who did not identify strongly with any of the preceding groups — though they tended to be apocalyptic in orientation.

Members of these groups engaged one another on the question of what was required for someone to be a faithful Jew. Indeed, open and frank debate was a mark of Judaism.

The geographical area in which Jesus lived is about the same as the present-day state of Israel. In the north was Galilee. Its population was about half gentile. Jewish people today often refer to this area as "the Galilee." Samaria was immediately south of Galilee and north of Jerusalem. Samaritans shared much of the same history as the Jewish people, but during the exile they developed their own scriptures, their own temple, their own priesthood, and some of their own customs. Their scriptures consisted of their own version of the books of Moses (Genesis, Exodus, Leviticus, Numbers, and Deuteronomy). Their temple was located on Mount Gerizim (rather than on Mount Zion, Jerusalem). Samaritans and Jewish people often coexisted peacefully, but from time to time animosity did break out between them. The third area was Judea — located between the Dead Sea and the Mediterranean Sea, with Jerusalem as its capital. Judea was the largest center of Jewish population in Palestine. The Romans often referred to Judea and Samaria by the one name Judea.

Although the Jewish people formed the largest population group in Judea, many gentiles lived harmoniously alongside Jews. Many Jewish people in Judea spoke both Aramaic and Greek. Many people lived at a subsistence level.

Jewish People outside of Judea

At the time of the New Testament, many Jewish people lived outside of Judea. This dispersion of the Jewish people is sometimes called the Diaspora. The Jewish population of Alexandria in Egypt was about 100,000. The map on p. 33 shows where Jewish people were concentrated. While Jewish people sometimes lived in Jewish neighborhoods, they interacted with gentiles every day. By and large these interactions were respectful and friendly. However, from time to time, some gentiles did exhibit prejudice against some Jewish people. In the early 50s C.E., for example, the Emperor Claudius expelled the Jewish people from the city of Rome. Claudius allowed the Jewish people of Rome to return after a few years.

The Jewish residents of the Diaspora spoke Greek and worshiped in a synagogue. A synagogue was a local Jewish community of worship, teaching, and mutual support, much like a Christian congregation is today. Like the people in Judea (just above), the Jewish people who lived in the dispersion had to figure out how much gentile culture to allow in the Jewish home and synagogue. Diaspora Jews struggled with how much gentile culture they could accept and when they had to say, "No. If we cross a certain line, we are no longer faithful." These struggles are the back story of some of the writings in the New Testament.

The Jewish population outside Judea passed on its Jewish heritage in the home and in the synagogue. Many Jewish children and young people went to schools sponsored by gentiles where they became acquainted with the teachings of Greek thinkers (such as Plato and Aristotle and their intellectual descendants). Furthermore, Jewish people in the Diaspora often came into contact with current and popular religious and philosophical ideas such as those of the Stoics and Epicureans.[2] Some New Testament writers borrowed words, ideas, and styles of writing from these Greek writers.

2. The Stoics were a school of Greek philosophy that was concerned with the active relationship between cosmic determinism and human freedom, and the belief that it is virtuous to maintain a will that is in accord with nature. Because of this, the Stoics presented their philosophy as a way of life, and they thought that the

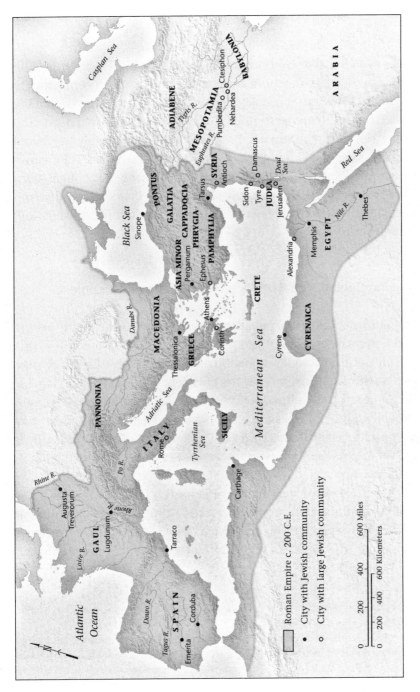

The Roman Empire and Jewish Population

33

In Judea and especially in the Diaspora, gentiles were sometimes attracted to the monotheism and high ethical standards of Judaism but were reluctant to convert to Judaism. Such gentiles were called "God-fearers" because they revered ("feared") the God of the Jews. The God-fearers attended the synagogue and lived according to the Ten Commandments. Some of these people evidently feared circumcision or did not want to follow the Jewish diet. They were a prime seedbed for the early Christian message: Through Jesus Christ, they could become full participants in a community connected to the God of the Jews. Many early gentile converts were God-fearers.

Leaving Behind Negative Pictures of the Jewish People

I close this chapter with an appeal. In an earlier time, many people had a negative picture of the Jewish people. In some corners, this picture continues today. Many Christians and non-Christians alike used to think of Judaism (and the Jewish people) as rigid and legalistic. Some Christians have accused the Jewish religion of works righteousness, that is, you have to work your way into God's favor. You have to do certain things for God to love you. To this day, I hear Christian preachers speak of the Pharisees in the New Testament in this way.

Such negative stereotypes contribute to prejudice against the Jewish people. At their worst, they lead to anti-Semitism, the systematic hatred of people who are Jewish. Anti-Semitism resulted in the Holocaust, the mass slaughter of 6,000,000 Jewish people during the Second World War.

---

best indication of an individual's philosophy was not what a person said but how he behaved.

Epicureans followed a system of philosophy based upon the teachings of Epicurus. Epicurus believed that the greatest good was to seek modest pleasures in order to attain a state of tranquility and freedom from fear, as well as absence of bodily pain through knowledge of the workings of the world and the limits of one's desires.

I hope the brief review of Judaism in this chapter reveals that this negative picture is wrong. Judaism seeks to promote the blessing of all people. At its best, Judaism is a religion of joy and grace. The commandments (laws) are not straitjackets but are guides for living as God wants. The time is long past for gentiles — whether Christian or not — to expose the negative picture of Jews and Judaism as a lie and to call for respect toward the Jewish community.

Judaism seeks to promote the blessing of all people. At its best, Judaism is a religion of joy and grace. The commandments (laws) are not straitjackets but are guides for living as God wants.

QUESTIONS FOR DISCUSSION

1. What would it have felt like to live in the Roman Empire? What do you think people in that world longed for?

2. Do you see similarities between the world of the Roman Empire and our world today? What do people long for in your social circles?

3. Can you name people or groups today who are similar to the Sadducees, the Zealots, the Pharisees, and the apocalyptic (end-time) group? With which group(s) do you most strongly identify?

4. The church today struggles with a question similar to that of Judaism, which was dispersed in the gentile world outside of Judea. What are some ways the church today is bringing aspects of the outside world into our worship, thinking, and behavior? Which values and behaviors from the culture at large should the church allow to come inside? Where should we draw the line?

5. The God-fearers were a natural audience for the early Christian message. Can you identify people today who are similar — who have a spiritual impulse but are reluctant to join the church? What might the church do to reach out to such people?

6. Negative caricatures of the Jewish people are not as widespread as they used to be. Nevertheless, I wonder if you can think of occasions when you have heard them. What would you do today if someone made an anti-Jewish remark or used a negative caricature of Jewish people in your presence?

CHAPTER 3

The Content of the New Testament: Two Mini-Surveys

My family's house is located along a flight path for the Indianapolis International Airport. Frequently I am on planes that pass over our neighborhood. From that elevation, I can see the big picture of our neighborhood — streets, houses, schools, churches, shopping areas, bike paths, parks, the state fairgrounds, and trails that wind across vacant lots and yards. From the airplane window, I can see things that I seldom notice when I am driving on the ground.

I hope this chapter helps you feel like you are in an airplane overlooking the neighborhood that is the New Testament as we overview the New Testament from two perspectives. (1) One survey tells the story of the events in the New Testament in the chronological order in which they happened. This approach may be more familiar to you than the next one. (2) The second survey tells the order in which the books of the New Testament were written. The letters of Paul were written before Matthew, Mark, Luke, and John. Much of the rest of the New Testament was written either at the same time as the Gospels or later than they. Box 5 relates the pivotal New Testament events to writings connected to those events.

Box 5. A Time Line of Events and Writings in the New Testament

Year	Event	New Testament Writing
4 B.C.E.	Birth of Jesus	
27-30 C.E.	Preaching of John the Baptist and his execution	
27-30	Ministry of Jesus	
30	Death, resurrection, and ascension of Jesus	
30ff.	Pentecost and life of the early Jerusalem community	
33-35	Call of Paul to be missionary to the gentiles	
33-64	Ministry of Paul (missionary journeys, founding and counseling congregations, death)	
49-51		Paul writes 1 Thessalonians, the earliest surviving Christian document
50-58		Paul writes his other books in about this order: Galatians 1 and 2 Corinthians Philippians Philemon Romans
61-64	Paul dies in Rome	
65-75		One of Paul's students writes Colossians
70	Romans conquer Jerusalem and destroy the temple	Mark
80-90		Matthew Luke and Acts (written by the same author) 1 Peter James Ephesians Jude
90-100		John 2 Thessalonians 2 Peter Revelation Hebrews
100-110		1 and 2 Timothy, Titus 1, 2, and 3 John

These dates are approximate. Scholars sometimes offer alternative dates.

Mini-Survey: The Events of the New Testament in the Order They Happened

You will not find these events listed in exactly this order in any one book in the New Testament. This list of events is compiled from a commonly accepted scholarly reconstruction augmented with information from books of the New Testament.

Each book tells a story in its own way and for its own purposes. To mesh the stories together is to confuse the authors' unique aims.

An important principle is that when you are working with a particular book of the New Testament, you need to pay attention to what is included (and not included) *in that book.* For example, when studying the Christmas story in Matthew, you look at the Christmas story *in Matthew.* Each book tells a story in its own way and for its own purposes. To mesh the stories together is to confuse the authors' unique aims. Nevertheless, this overview can help develop a sense of the order of major events.

The Birth of Jesus (4 B.C.E.)

Jesus was born to Joseph and Mary. While we often think that that event took place in the year 0, most scholars believe it occurred in the year 4 B.C.E. In the New Testament, the birth of Jesus is narrated briefly only by Matthew and Luke (Matthew 1:18–2:12; Luke 1:5–2:40). We know little about Jesus' childhood and youth, though Luke says that at the age of 12, Jesus dialogued with the leaders of the temple (Luke 2:41-52).

John the Baptist (25-30 C.E.)

John the Baptist (the son of Elizabeth and Zechariah) was an end-time preacher whom Luke describes as a cousin of Jesus. John was an apocalyptic preacher who believed that God was about to destroy the present world and bring about a new one. John sought to alert people to the coming destruction and to urge people to prepare for it by repentance and baptism. John's ministry took place about 25-30 C.E.

The Ministry of Jesus (27 to 30 C.E.)

Jesus is the central character in the New Testament. The New Testament focuses on how God operated through Jesus. Scholars are uncertain as to whether the ministry of Jesus lasted only a few months (about the year 30 C.E.) or as long as three years (about 27 to 30 C.E.). According to Luke, Jesus was about thirty years of age when he began his formal ministry (Luke 3:23). Although thirty years seems relatively young by today's standards, it was closer to middle age at the time of Jesus.

In the next chapter we will summarize the ministry of Jesus more fully. Here it is enough to note that his primary message was similar to that of John the Baptist: God is about to destroy the present evil age and bring about a new world, called the Realm of God. We sometimes speak of Jesus' ministry having three prongs:

- Preaching, that is, announcing the presence and future of the Realm of God.
- Teaching, that is, explaining the Realm of God and guiding people in how to live faithfully in response.
- Working miracles, that is, demonstrating the partial presence of the Realm of God in the present.

Jesus gathered twelve close followers (disciples or apostles), the most well known of whom were Peter and James. The Jewish world was one of intense dialogue and debate. Jesus entered into such dialogue with the Pharisees (see p. 30) and others. The Romans put Jesus to death by crucifying him.

The Gospel of John presents a slightly different view of Jesus (discussed in the next chapter). For John, Jesus is God's revealer come down from heaven. This picture is seldom in conflict with the one in Matthew, Mark, and Luke, but it is different.

Resurrection and Ascension (30 c.e.)

The crucifixion took place at mid-day on a Friday. By sundown, Jesus' disciples had placed his body in a tomb that was carved as a cave in a rock face. On the following Sunday morning, according to the Gospel writers, God raised Jesus back to life, and Jesus appeared to his followers. According to the Gospel writers his body was not simply resuscitated but was transformed. For Mark, Matthew, and Luke, the resurrection was proof that the Realm of God was for real and that Jesus was its agent.

According to the book of Acts, after the resurrection Jesus ascended into heaven. He left the earth and was lifted upward into heaven (Acts 1:1-11). Several New Testament writers emphasize that in heaven Jesus is at God's right hand, where he rules over the rulers of the earth.

The Second Coming (A Hope for the Future)

The most important event discussed in the New Testament has not yet occurred. Many New Testament authors believed that Jesus would return from heaven to end the present age and to complete the coming of the Realm of God. This event is often called "the Second Coming," although that phrase does not actually appear in the New Testament itself. Several writers in the New Testament attempted to encourage their readers to continue living faithfully toward the hope of that return (for example, Mark 13:32-37; Matthew 24:36-44; Luke 21:34-36).

Pentecost (30 C.E.)

The next major event after the resurrection and ascension, according to the book of Acts, was the coming of the Holy Spirit on the Day of Pentecost. Pentecost was a Jewish religious festival that celebrated the beginning of the harvest. After telling about the ascension, the book of Acts recounts that a large group of disciples was in Jerusalem at the time of the Pentecost festival, uncertain about what they were to do. God sent the Holy Spirit upon them like a mighty wind. In the New Testament, as in the Old, the Holy Spirit is one of God's closest agents. Although it is invisible, the Spirit brings God's power to life. The Holy Spirit filled the disciples with power to become a community whose purpose was to witness to the coming of the Realm of God. The Gospel of John gives its own version of the coming of the Spirit (John 20:22).

The Holy Spirit filled the disciples with power to become a community whose purpose was to witness to the coming of the Realm of God.

Earliest Followers of Jesus in Jerusalem (30-70 C.E.)

After Pentecost, the disciples lived in close community in Jerusalem. They not only provided personal encouragement, but they also supported one another financially. Peter emerged as a leader of this group, with James as a close associate. This largely Jewish community sought to alert their friends and neighbors to the Realm of God. As far as we know, they did not encourage people to leave Judaism. Instead, they saw themselves as a group within Judaism with the particular purpose of trying to prepare people for the end of the old world and the beginning of the new. They did not see themselves establishing a new religion but saw themselves as an extension of Judaism. They saw themselves as an end-time community witnessing to the presence of the Realm in the present.

42

The Call of Paul (33 c.e.) and His Early Ministry

About the year 33, a Jewish leader named Paul was harassing some followers of Jesus. However, both Paul's own writings and the book of Acts assert that God called Paul to become a missionary to the gentiles. The church was already welcoming gentiles into its end-time community, but Paul now had a particular mission to carry the news of the coming of God's Realm to the gentiles. On these journeys, Paul preached, taught, and established congregations. He also raised funds for the congregation in Jerusalem. Paul invited gentiles to come into the end-time community without also being initiated into Judaism.

Paul now had a particular mission to carry the news of the coming of God's Realm to the gentiles.

Paul's story is told in two places in the New Testament — in letters that come from Paul's own hand, and in the book of Acts. These two versions share much in common, but they also contain some differences (discussed in Chapter 6 below).

The Jerusalem Council (47 c.e.)

Some tensions developed between the church in Jerusalem and Paul and the congregations that he founded. The main issue was whether the gentiles who came into Paul's churches needed to convert to Judaism (including circumcision, following the Jewish dietary pattern, and otherwise living in the Jewish way). The leaders of the Jerusalem congregation met with Paul to discuss this issue. Together they agreed that the gentiles had full standing without being initiated into Judaism. Henceforth, the Jerusalem church would concentrate its mission on the Jewish community while Paul would continue to focus on gentiles.[1]

1. As we note in Chapter 6, the book of Acts and the letter to the Galatians present two slightly different versions of this resolution.

Paul's Later Ministry (47-62 C.E.)

After the Jerusalem Council, Paul resumed his traveling ministry, founding and tending congregations. During this period, he wrote the seven letters that are definitely from his own hand (1 Thessalonians, Galatians, 1 and 2 Corinthians, Philippians, Philemon, and Romans). Paul wrote in response to tensions that developed within the congregations. The struggles varied from congregation to congregation, ranging from believers losing hope in the Second Coming (1 Thessalonians) through internal division (the Corinthian correspondence) to gentile disrespect for Judaism (Romans). Paul also took up a collection for the church in Jerusalem. Paul was imprisoned for a time, perhaps in Ephesus. By the end of his life (about 62-64 C.E.), Paul had visited places such as Philippi, Thessalonica, Corinth, Ephesus, Macedonia, and Galatia. He revisited Jerusalem, eventually reaching Rome, where he was executed at the time of the infamous Nero Caesar.

Two Generations of Paul's Students (65-110 C.E.)

After Paul's death, the congregations that he founded and those in the Pauline tradition not only continued, but continued to have internal difficulties. Using Paul's name, followers of Paul wrote to some of these congregations. Although writing in someone else's name may sound like forgery today, it was an accepted practice in the ancient world for students of prominent leaders to extend the leader's teaching to a new situation by writing in that person's name. The first generation of Paul's students probably wrote Colossians and Ephesians in this way. The second (or third) generation wrote 2 Thessalonians as well as 1 and 2 Timothy and Titus.

Box 6. The Authorship of the Letters

To be sure, a good many scholars think that Paul wrote all the letters that bear his name. However, scholars who think that Paul wrote some of the letters that bear his name while Paul's followers wrote others do so on the following grounds. Some of the vocabulary and grammar is a little different in the two sets of letters. More importantly, the interpretation of Jesus and other theological matters in the two bodies of literature is expressed with different nuances. The organization of the churches appears to be more highly developed in the later letters than in the seven letters certainly from Paul's own hand. Scholars who follow this line of analysis are divided over whether Colossians and Ephesians are genuinely from Paul. Virtually all scholars in this camp think that one of Paul's disciples wrote 2 Thessalonians as well as 1 and 2 Timothy and Titus.

In one respect, the matter of authorship is not a central concern to the church. The Christian community continues to find all of the letters attributed to Paul to be valuable conversation partners in helping to discern God's presence and purposes. In another respect, however, the question of authorship is important. If the interpreter thinks that Paul wrote all of the letters that appear to come from his hand, the interpreter can use all of those letters to interpret the thought of Paul. However, if the interpreter thinks that Paul wrote only the seven undisputed epistles, then when speaking about *Paul,* the interpreter should focus only on those epistles. The interpreter can then compare Paul's thought with that in the other letters and can trace trajectories of theological development.

The Destruction of the Temple (70 C.E.)

When a Roman procurator (governor) stole money from the temple treasury in the year 66 C.E., some Jewish people revolted against Rome. The Roman government cracked down with powerful military force. War between the Jewish people and the Romans continued from 66 to 70, with the climax coming when the Romans devastated the temple and destroyed much of Jerusalem in 70 C.E. A time of social unrest followed. The temple was one of the most important symbols of Judaism, and its destruction created a massive crisis in Judaism. Many Jewish institutions — including the temple — were no longer in operation. Jerusalem, and much of Judea, was in ruins and/or social chaos. Many groups — such as the priests and the Sadducees — lost power. The community was haunted by questions such as, Why did God allow the temple to be destroyed? What would be the future of Judaism? One of the big questions facing the Jewish community was how to reorganize in the wake of the destruction of so many of their institutions.

Several books of the New Testament were written — in part — to respond to issues raised by the destruction of the temple. You can find hints that this calamity had already occurred in some of the materials in the New Testament written after the year 70 C.E. (for example, Mark 13:1-2; Luke 13:31-35; 19:41-44; 21:20-24).

Jesus' Followers Cast out of a Small
Group of Synagogues (90 C.E.)

In many communities in the Mediterranean world, Jesus' followers and traditional Jewish people got along quite well. In fact, some of Jesus' followers participated as full members of synagogues until at least the fourth century C.E. However, there were tensions between the two groups in some areas, and according to John 9:22 and 34, at least a small group of synagogues excommunicated followers of Jesus from their fellowship. The Gospel of John, and perhaps the letters of John, were partly written in response to this event. John sought to assure his readers that they were fully and faithfully Jewish even as they believed in Jesus.

Other Writings and Events (80 C.E. to 100 C.E.)

The writings of the New Testament that we have not mentioned so far also came into existence in response to particular issues, questions, and circumstances. These situations are mentioned briefly in the mini-survey that follows.

An important development comes into play. The Roman Emperor Domitian, who ruled from 80 to 96 C.E., claimed a more elevated divine status than the previous emperors, even speaking of himself as "Lord and God." The book of Revelation was written, in no small part, to criticize this flagrant idolatry as well as the general exploitation and violence of the Roman Empire.

Mini-Survey: The Books of the New Testament in the Order They Were Written

Few of the books of the New Testament were written for general circulation. Most were addressed to particular congregations. Indeed, the authors of the New Testament did not write their books simply to make a record. The writers of the New Testament took quills in hand to respond to issues in particular congregations. Most of the authors of the New Testament wrote to help congregations deal with problems.

None of the books of the New Testament would have been written if the early churches had not had conflicts regarding what to believe and how to live.

Indeed, none of the books of the New Testament would have been written if the early churches had not had conflicts regarding what to believe and how to live.[2]

---

2. I largely follow the dating in Dennis E. Smith, ed., *Chalice Introduction to the New Testament* (St. Louis: Chalice Press, 2004), esp. pp. 28-30.

I now turn to a mini-survey of the books of the New Testament in the approximate order in which they were written. I say "approximate" because scholars do not always agree when particular books were written.

1 Thessalonians (49-51 C.E.). The book of 1 Thessalonians is the first book written among those we possess. People in Thessalonica had begun to lose hope in the Second Coming, so Paul wrote to encourage them to continue to live faithfully in spite of the delay of that event.

Galatians (55 C.E.). The Galatian congregation was divided over whether gentiles who converted to the God of Israel through Jesus Christ needed also to be initiated fully into Judaism. Paul affirmed that gentiles had full standing in the church without being circumcised or otherwise subject to matters of Jewish law or custom.

1 and 2 Corinthians (53-57 C.E.). The congregation at Corinth was divided over many issues including sexual behavior, food that had been offered to idols, speaking in tongues in public worship, the bodily resurrection, questions about the validity of Paul's apostleship, the need for the congregation to give to the offering for the church in Jerusalem, and how to respond to the "super apostles" who had come into the community.

Philippians (56 C.E.). Paul was not the only missionary in the ancient church. Paul wrote Philippians while he was imprisoned to assure the congregation of his well-being and to warn them against false teachers ("dogs") who had visited Philippi.

Philemon (56 C.E.). Paul wrote this letter to an individual, Philemon, whose slave (Onesimus) had escaped and fled to Paul. Paul sent Onesimus back to Philemon with the admonition that Philemon receive the slave as a brother.

Romans (58 C.E.). I am convinced that the problem in the Roman congregations was that gentile Christians disrespected the Jewish people (both those in the church and traditional Jewish people). Paul urges the gentiles to respect Jewish people.[3]

---

3. There is a spectrum of interpretations for the book of Romans, with three main approaches today. (1) My own view, as stated above, is that Paul urges the gen-

Colossians (65-75 C.E.). False teachers taught this congregation that they needed to deny themselves certain things (asceticism), observe special holy days, and worship celestial powers to gain access to God. The writer, a student of Paul, assures readers that God's work through Christ has already opened access to God.

Mark (70 C.E.). Mark wrote the second Gospel immediately after the Romans destroyed the temple in Jerusalem (70 C.E.). Mark's community was confused, fearful, and losing faith. Mark interprets the burning of the temple as a sign that the end of the world was near and that Jesus would soon return.

Matthew (80-90 C.E.). The congregation to whom Matthew wrote was both uncertain about whether Jesus would return and about the relationship between Jesus and Judaism and the gentile mission. Matthew presents Jesus as a rabbi whose principal teaching was about the end time and how to live in preparation for it.

---

tiles to respect the Jewish members of the congregations. A small but growing number of scholars follows this view. (2) At the other end of the interpretive spectrum is an influential traditional view (associated especially with Martin Luther). According to this perspective, the fundamental problem with which Romans deals is how an individual is saved. From this perspective, Judaism taught that one can be saved through good works, that being obedient to the law is the means to win God's favor. This interpretation of Jewish salvation is sometimes called works-righteousness. According to these interpreters, Paul writes Romans to reject this "Jewish" view. By contrast, human beings are saved through the grace revealed in Jesus Christ. Grace releases us from the burden of having to do enough works to win God's approval. This view is anti-Jewish at its core. A small and shrinking group of scholars follows this perspective. (3) Between these two poles is a middle view, sometimes called "the new perspective on Paul," that sees Paul's thinking as deriving from Judaism in a positive way. The new perspective rejects the idea that Judaism was a religion of works-righteousness. Jewish leaders did expect converts to adopt Jewish practices such as circumcision and the dietary customs, not as works to prove worth to God, but more as badges of identity. The new element that Paul introduces is seeing Jesus as the apocalyptic turning point of the ages and as the means through which God is now welcoming gentiles into the church. Paul wrote Romans because Jewish and gentile members of the congregation at Rome were not living in community. Paul does not criticize Judaism as a religion but does chide the Jewish members of the congregation to welcome gentiles as full members of the church without asking the gentiles to assume the badges (such as circumcision and practicing the dietary customs) that continue to be appropriate for Jewish people.

Luke and *Acts* (80-90 C.E.). We should read and study these two books together because they tell one story. The church to which they were directed was losing confidence in the Second Coming and struggled with welcoming gentiles without requiring them to convert to Judaism. The congregation also struggled with disparity between the rich and the poor and with authority. According to these

---

Box 7. The Importance of the Temple

Although Christians sometimes speak casually of "the" temple, that building had three lives. Solomon oversaw the construction of the first temple in the tenth century B.C.E. Solomon's temple was a spectacular architectural specimen. The Babylonians destroyed this temple in 587/586 B.C.E. In the sixth century B.C.E. a second temple was built on the foundations of the first one. Later, Herod, Roman puppet governor of Palestine, enlarged and remodeled the second temple to such an extent that it was sometimes regarded as a third temple, "Herod's Temple." While the Romans destroyed much of the third temple in 70 C.E., some of its massive foundation stones survive. Today they are often known as the Wailing Wall, and people pray before them.

While biblical writers sometimes spoke as if God dwelled in the temple, they did not mean that God dwelled only in the temple. Indeed, according to the best Jewish theology God is omnipresent, that is, God is present at every moment in every place (e.g., Psalm 139:7-12). Nevertheless, the temple was a powerful symbol of the divine presence and promises. The destruction of the temple raised searching theological questions for the Jewish community (for such questions, see p. 46).

Mark, Matthew, and Luke interpreted the destruction of the temple in 70 C.E. as a sign that the end times were at hand (Mark 13:14-20; Matthew 24:15-28; Luke 21:20-24). The Gospel writers encouraged their congregations to remain faithful even in the chaos in Judaism following the destruction of the temple.

---

books, God sent the Spirit on Pentecost to empower the church during the delay in the Second Coming.

1 Peter (80-90 C.E.). The congregation to whom this letter was directed was made up of gentiles who had converted to Christian faith and whose former gentile friends ridiculed them. They perceived themselves as strangers or exiles. Although this document bears the name of the apostle Peter, few scholars today think that he was the author. The person who wrote in Peter's name urged the recipients to see their suffering as similar to that of Jesus and to behave toward one another and toward others in ways that would win the approval of their detractors.

James (80-90 C.E.). The congregation to whom James was written was not living out their faith. They did such things as show favoritism toward the wealthy (while neglecting the poor) and engaging in backbiting and gossip. The author is said to be James, a brother of Jesus, but this is unlikely. The author reminds the community that faith without works (living in covenant with one another in community) is dead.

Ephesians (80-90 C.E.). Many scholars think that Ephesians was written not to one congregation but to several different congregations. The writer, a follower of Paul, speaks to gentiles to clarify the fact that through Christ they have been adopted into the hope of Israel and the coming Realm of God. In consequence, they are to live in covenant with one another to embody the new life.

Jude (80-90 C.E.). The congregation to whom this tiny letter was directed had been visited by people who claimed to be prophets freed from moral restrictions, especially in regard to sexual behavior. Jude firmly states that Jesus' followers are to live lives that demonstrate appropriate restraint.

John (90-100 C.E.). As we noted above, the members of the congregation to whom the Gospel of John was written had previously been participants in a synagogue. However, they had recently been cast out of the synagogue. John wrote to reinforce their confidence that they were faithfully Jewish while believing in Jesus.

2 Thessalonians (90-100 C.E.). Whereas 1 Thessalonians portrays the Second Coming of Jesus occurring right away, 2 Thessalonians recognizes that a lot of time will pass before Jesus' return. Consequently, the church needs to live obediently during the delay. While attributed to Paul, this writing was likely penned by one of Paul's followers.

2 Peter (90-100 C.E.). The community receiving this letter was influenced by people who claimed that Christians were free from traditional Jewish moral boundaries. Such freedom made it possible for them to move easily in gentile society. However, the author retorts that Christ will return as judge to condemn those who abandon traditional ethical norms.

Book of Revelation (90-95 C.E.). The congregations to which this book was written were either being persecuted or were fearful of being persecuted by the mighty Roman Empire. The author wrote to help the people see that the violence and idolatry of the empire would lead to its destruction and would set the stage for the coming of the new world. Therefore, the members of the congregation should endure their difficult times.

Hebrews (90-100 C.E.). This book is very likely an early Christian sermon written for a congregation that had suffered under persecution. Their confidence that Jesus provided a way for salvation had been challenged. Some people were drifting away from their faith. The unnamed preacher exhorts them to remember that Jesus had walked a similar path. Their own suffering was a temporary discomfort on the path to salvation.

1 and 2 Timothy and Titus (100-110 C.E.). These books are sometimes called "the pastoral epistles" because their author sees him- or herself as a pastor (or shepherd). False teachers have visited the community; therefore, the writer (in the name of Paul) sets out clear guidelines for recognizing authentic leaders (bishops and deacons) and for managing community life (for example, caring for widows and avoiding unnecessary self-denial).

1, 2, and 3 John (100-110 C.E.). These three letters were written by the same author as the Gospel of John but to a different situation. The writer now seeks to correct some people who have left the community and who have adopted unsatisfactory views of Jesus and of the faithful life.

A Sign of Hope: Written for Questioning, Struggling People

On the one hand, each book of the New Testament was written to a distinct situation and put forward its own message. On the other hand, similar themes run through many of these books. Common concerns of New Testament authors include understanding the relationship between Judaism and Jesus' followers, persevering through difficult times while awaiting the Second Coming of Jesus, abiding by the characteristics of the faithful life, and a concern with avoiding false teachers and recognizing trustworthy teaching. I am reassured by the fact that virtually every document in the New Testament was written in response to problems in local communities. As a practicing Christian, I sometimes get discouraged by the behavior of the church. The books of the New Testament were written to encourage people who had questions and who struggled much as we do today. The fact that the church is still here with its questions and struggles is a sign of hope.

The books of the New Testament were written to encourage people who had questions and who struggled much as we do today.

QUESTIONS FOR DISCUSSION

1. Were you surprised as you read the mini-survey of the books of the New Testament in the order they were written?
2. When you start to read a passage of the New Testament, it is useful to take account of when events described in the book took place, the order in which they occurred, and when the book itself was written. As an example, take Jesus' prediction of the destruction of the temple in Luke 21:20-24. What does awareness of each of those time lines prompt you to ask and think about this passage?
3. How does understanding how the New Testament developed (described in the last part of the chapter) help you think about the New Testament?
4. What questions has this little survey sparked for you?

CHAPTER 4

The Story of Jesus

Before reading further, I suggest that you take a moment and write down what you think was the core of Jesus' message. What were his most important values? What did he most want people to do? You can then use your sketch as a point of comparison and contrast while reading this chapter.

Often we like to imagine not only that Jesus looks like us, but also that Jesus was a first-century version of ourselves.

People of European origin often portray Jesus with long, brown hair and beard, European features, and a glow around his face. Others sometimes picture him as an African American, a Latino, or an Asian. The truth, of course, is that we do not know for sure how Jesus looked, except that he had the features of a Mediterranean Jewish peasant.

Often we like to imagine not only that Jesus looks like us, but also that Jesus was a first-century version of ourselves. Advocates of conservative politics may think of Jesus as a first-century Republican. To liberal Democrats Jesus may be "blue." For some socialists, Jesus was the first Marxist.

Jesus, of course, was a person of the first century. This chapter summarizes the ministry of Jesus (as I see it).[1] Chapter 8 focuses on

---

1. To be fair, I note that the interpretation of Jesus in this book is only one of several ways of reconstructing the message and mission of Jesus.

how Matthew, Mark, Luke, and John interpret the story of Jesus after the Romans destroyed the temple in Jerusalem.

The Big Idea in the Background of Jesus' Ministry: The Realm of God

A big idea lies behind the teaching of Jesus and the writings of Paul, Matthew, Mark, Luke, and most other writers of the New Testament: the Realm of God. According to this idea, accepted by many people of Jesus' day, history was divided into four eras.

1. In paradise (the Garden of Eden), everything took place according to God's designs for love, peace, and abundance.
2. Human beings disobeyed God, which caused God to curse humankind and the earth (the fall).
3. History continued as an extended time marked by the presence of Satan, demons, idolatry, fractiousness among peoples (especially between Jewish and gentile communities), injustice, poverty, sickness, fracture with the natural world, violence, and death.
4. Because God promised blessing, God would destroy the present evil age with a massive historical interruption (an apocalypse) and set in place the Realm of God — a new world in which God and the angels ruled fully and which would be marked by mutuality, support, justice, health, blessing between humankind and nature, peace, and eternal life. In the Realm of God, the Jewish and gentile communities would be reunited in one great human family.

People become part of the Realm of God, according to John the Baptist and Jesus who echoed him, by repenting and being baptized. Those who do not repent but continue to collude with the powers and values of the old age God condemns to a fiery punishment (hell).

John the Baptist Prepared the Way

All four Gospel writers use John the Baptist to introduce the ministry of Jesus. John was an end-time prophet who sought to prepare people for the coming of the Realm of God by repentance and baptism. To repent was to turn away from things that deny God's purposes (for example, idolatry, injustice, and violence) and to turn toward the values of God (for example, justice, peace, and love). Baptism was a rite in which people were immersed in water to represent washing away the old world and being born into the Realm of God. John baptized Jesus. This indicates that Jesus shared John's perspective on the end of time and the coming of the Realm of God. John wore clothing of camel hair that Jews in his day would have associated with the prophets of old, and he lived an ascetic lifestyle (eating only honey and locusts) — again akin to the prophets. John's preaching unnerved Herod Antipas (whom the Romans appointed to rule Galilee and Perea), who had John beheaded.

Box 8. John the Baptist

To read further about John the Baptist, see Matthew 3:1-17; 11:2-19; 14:1-12; Mark 1:1-11; 6:14-29; Luke 1:57-80; 3:1-22; 9:7-9. Here is a sample of John's preaching: "You brood of vipers! Who warned you to flee from the wrath to come? Bear fruits worthy of repentance" (Matt. 3:7-8 and Luke 3:7-8).

The Preaching of Jesus Announced the Realm of God

In many documents in antiquity, the first words that a character speaks are very important. In the Gospel of Mark, Jesus begins with: "The time is fulfilled, and the kingdom [Realm] of God is at hand; repent and believe in the good news" (Mark 1:15). The first part of this expression means that the time has come for God to bring the Realm in its fullness. Jesus' listeners are to respond by repenting and believing in that good news.[2] Jesus' opening words are a little different in Matthew and Luke, but they mean the same thing.

According to the earliest traditions about Jesus — and according to their later interpretations in Matthew, Mark, and Luke — the Realm of God is not only *about* to come — in the future — but is already *partially manifest* in the present through the ministry of Jesus. The work of Jesus not only pointed to the coming of the Realm in the future but brought it to life in a limited way in the present. The earliest churches expected the Realm of God to appear in its completeness only when Jesus returned from heaven.

> **The Realm of God is not only *about* to come — in the future — but is already *partially manifest* in the present through the ministry of Jesus.**

The Teaching of Jesus Explained the Realm and How to Live in Light of It

Jesus not only announced the presence and coming of the Realm, but the teaching of Jesus explained the Realm and helped his hearers respond to it. Jesus explains that when people become aware of the presence and coming of the Realm, they should re-order their lives around it. People should not only prepare for the future coming of the Realm by repenting and being baptized, but should also live out the values of the Realm day to day in the present. This means turning away from idolatry and living in peace, in mutuality, in support, in forgiveness, in justice — in both personal and social relationships — in joining with Jesus' healing ministry, in sharing mate-

---

2. The words "good news" are from a Greek word that means "good news." This word is often translated "gospel." While the general meaning of the word "gospel" is "good news," in the New Testament it usually refers specifically to the good news of God's redeeming work through Jesus Christ. Different New Testament authors have slightly different understandings of that work.

rial resources so that all people live in abundance, in respect for creation, and in the hope of eternal life.

As you run across Jesus' teaching in Matthew, Mark, and Luke, you should ask yourself: How does this teaching help people understand and respond to the Realm of God?

Jesus taught using different methods, one of the best known of which are the parables. Parables are short stories designed to surprise the hearer into recognizing the presence of the Realm of God breaking into this world. For instance, the parable of the Good Samaritan (discussed further in Chapter 12) reveals that even the least savory character can behave in a way that reveals the Realm of God. Jesus also taught in prose, explaining his ministry, the law, and the meaning of the Realm of God. Jesus also taught with short, memorable sayings.

Let me show you an example in which Jesus' teaching on the Realm of God can help us understand his message. In Matthew 5:21-26, Jesus said, "You have heard that it was said to those of ancient times, 'You shall not murder'; and 'whoever murders shall be liable to judgment.' But I say to you that if you are angry with a brother or sister, you will be liable to judgment." Jesus goes on to teach that if you become aware that your sister or brother has something against you, you should be reconciled with that person. From the point of view of the Realm, God wants all people to live together in supportive relationships. Murder destroys a relationship altogether. According to this text, anger destroys relationships in a way similar to murder. In the Realm of God all relationships are to have the supportive quality they had in the Garden of Eden. Consequently, Jesus instructs his followers to take steps to reconcile, that is, to confront the reasons that have prompted the anger and to resolve those issues. In the end, those who have failed to restore relationships risk being cast into hell.

Jesus also taught through his actions. For example, as we noted in the previous chapter, many Jewish people in the first century particularly looked down on tax collectors — Jewish people who contributed to the oppression of other Jewish people by collecting unfairly high taxes for the Roman Empire. However, Jesus ate with tax collectors to show that God welcomes into his Realm even those whom the world despises (see, for example, Matthew 9:10-13).[3]

The Miracles of Jesus Demonstrated the Presence of the Realm

Jesus performed four kinds of miracles. Each kind of miracle demonstrated that the Realm of God was present in Jesus and his ministry and revealed the character of that Realm. (1) *Healing of the sick:* These miracles showed that in the Realm, God would return people to health. For example, Jesus healed a woman who had had an issue of blood (probably vaginal bleeding) for twelve years and said to her: "your faith has healed you" (Mark 5:24-34). (2) *Casting demons* out of people (exorcisms): Jesus showed that God would vanquish the power of Satan and the demons and would fully restore people to their personal and social worlds. For instance, Jesus cast the demons out of a demoniac — a person possessed by demons — who lived in a tomb (Mark 5:1-20). Jesus told the man, who was overflowing with gratitude, to tell his people "how much the Lord ha[d] done for [him]."[4] (3) *Power over the destructive forces of nature* (such as storms): These miracles evidence that in the Realm of God, nature and humankind would live together in harmony. For example, Jesus calmed the storm-tossed sea (Mark 4:35-41). (4) *Raising the dead:* Jesus showed that God triumphed over the ultimate power of the devil and the old age. For instance, Jesus raised a twelve-year-old young woman who had died of an illness (Mark 5:21-24, 35-43).

---

3. In Judea, the Romans appointed Jewish people to collect the Roman taxes. The tax collectors (sometimes called publicans) thus functioned as agents of the Roman occupation and oppression. Furthermore, many tax collectors collected not only the amount that Rome required but freely extorted much more in order to fatten their own incomes. As a result, many people despised tax collectors.

4. People in antiquity believed that God's great adversary, Satan, had assistants called demons. The demons inhabited individuals, partially controlling them and leading them into destructive behavior.

Jesus in Discussion and Debate with His Contemporaries

I have already mentioned that the Jewish people of Jesus' day actively discussed their burning issues, especially those that pertained to living faithfully in the context of the Roman occupation and the wider oppressive conditions of the old world. Discussion often turned into debate, and the debates could be quite energetic. Such discussions often generated high-powered rhetoric, though (as far as I can tell) people then tended not to take such talk as personally as we tend to do today.

All of the Gospels present Jesus as entering into such discussions, especially with the Pharisees, the scribes, the Sadducees, and the priests. However, many scholars have come to a surprising conclusion about a good number of these vignettes. Many scholars think that the Gospel writers have lifted Jesus' words from the context in which he spoke and embroidered them into the fabric of their own time so that Jesus' words would speak to the emerging tensions between the Christian congregations — for whom the Gospels were written — and the traditional synagogues. The Gospel writers heightened the negative responses of the Jewish people to Jesus in their retelling. This literary ploy was intended to make Jesus and his followers look good over against the Jewish people. This was one way the early Christian writers helped create a separate identity between Jesus (and his followers) and traditional Judaism.

The Gospel writers sometimes cast the Jewish people in a very negative light. For example, they sometimes describe Pharisees and others as hypocrites. In Matthew Jesus refers to the Pharisees not only as "hypocrites" but also as "blind guides" and "whitewashed tombs" (Matthew 23:13, 16, 27). Most scholars think that these descriptions are exaggerations that the Gospel writers used to help justify the deepening divide between followers of Jesus and traditional Judaism. While this development is understandable from the perspective of that time, such stereotyping has had the tragic consequence of contributing to anti-Semitism. Today's reader needs to respect these passages as products of their own moment in history but

61

not use them as lenses for interpreting Judaism itself in either the past or the present.

The Death of Jesus

Jesus was crucified about the year 30 C.E. Christians have sometimes thought that the Jewish people killed Jesus. However, the Roman government did not grant the power of execution to the Jewish people. Rome alone had that power. The main reason the Romans put people to death was sedition — the charge that a person represented a threat to the power of the state. The Romans used public crucifixion as a means of controlling civil unrest by eliminating people who might be potential leaders of political disturbances, thereby warning others of the fate that would await all who threatened the state.

Jesus was arrested and tried before the Roman procurator, a regional ruler named Pontius Pilate.[5] Pilate was mostly concerned with whether Jesus had called himself "King of the Jews." Was Jesus someone who wished to depose Herod, whom the Romans had appointed to rule Palestine, or would he instigate revolt against Rome[6] (Matthew 27:37; Luke 23:38)? The Romans may have understood Jesus' announcement that the Realm of God is coming as an announcement that a Jewish revolt was about to begin.

> **The Romans may have understood Jesus' announcement that the Realm of God is coming as an announcement that a Jewish revolt was about to begin.**

The act of crucifixion was horrible. A cross consisted of an up-

5. According to the Gospels, after his arrest Jesus was questioned before a Jewish governing body called the Sanhedrin. While such an event may have occurred in history, the Gospel writers played up the role the Jewish leadership played and the venom it expressed toward Jesus. This, too, was a part of the Gospel writers' impulse described in the previous section to discredit some Jewish leaders since these may have been a problem for the young Christian group.

6. On the motif of "King of the Jews" see Matthew 27:11-13, 24-31; Mark 15:1-18; Luke 23:32-38.

right pole and a crossbeam. The place of crucifixion contained a small hole. Sometimes the victim carried the crossbeam from the courtroom to the place of execution, as Jesus did. When the victim approached the site, the upright pole would be lying on the ground. The crossbeam was attached to the upright, and the victim lay on the cross so that the executioners could drive nails in the wrists and ankles to hold the body on the cross. The cross was then lifted into the air and planted in the small hole. People stood around, watching. Death took place by asphyxiation as the weight of the body gradually collapsed the lungs. Since this process sometimes lasted several days, the fact that Jesus died in three hours was relatively merciful.

The Resurrection and Ascension of Jesus

As we noted previously, the resurrection of Jesus was a key demonstration of the coming of the Realm of God in the present and a foretaste of what life will be in God's Realm. Jesus had a resurrected body that characterized the Realm of God. In raising Jesus from the dead, God gave us a sneak peek at what our human bodies will be like when the Realm of God is fully present. The human body, like Jesus' resurrection body, is physical but also no longer prone to decay. Human bodies will not get old and die. Scholars sometimes refer to it as a resurrection body. The New Testament's fullest description of a resurrection body is found in 1 Corinthians 15:40-44:

> There are both heavenly bodies and earthly bodies, but the glory of the heavenly is one thing, and that of the earthly is another. There is one glory of the sun, and another glory of the moon, and another glory of the stars; indeed, star differs from star in glory.
>
> So it is with the resurrection of the dead. What is sown is perishable, what is raised is imperishable. It is sown in dishonor, it is raised in glory. It is sown in weakness, it is raised in power. It is sown a physical body, it is raised a spiritual body.

The resurrected Jesus had such a body.

As we mentioned in the previous chapter, the book of Acts describes the risen Jesus ascending from earth to heaven: "He was lifted up, and a cloud took him out of their sight" (Acts 1:6-11). According to Acts, when Jesus reached heaven, he took a place at the right hand of God (Acts 2:33-34; 7:55-56). While the book of Acts is the only book in the New Testament to narrate the ascension itself, other books state that the risen Jesus was at the right hand of God. For example, the book of Ephesians states that God raised Jesus "from the dead and seated him at [God's] right hand in the heavenly places" (Ephesians 1:20).

By picturing Jesus ascended to God's right hand, the New Testament writers imply that Jesus is God's agent to rule the earth.

Box 9. Texts in the New Testament That Depict Jesus at the Right Hand of God

Here are some texts that speak of the risen Jesus being at the right hand of God: Matthew 26:64; Mark 14:62; Luke 22:69; Acts 2:33-34; 5:31; 7:55-56; Romans 8:34; Ephesians 1:20; Colossians 3:1; Hebrews 1:3; 8:1; 10:12; 12:2; 1 Peter 3:22. For example, "God put this power [the power of the resurrection] to work in Christ when he raised him from the dead and seated him at his right hand in the heavenly places, far above all rule and authority and power and dominion, and above every name that is named, not only in this age but also in the age to come" (Ephesians 1:20-21).

In antiquity, the right hand was the hand of power and authority. By picturing Jesus ascended to God's right hand, the New Testament writers imply that Jesus is God's agent to rule the earth. The implication is that all other rulers — including Caesar — are ultimately subject to God. The Realm of God through Jesus will replace all other realms.

QUESTIONS FOR DISCUSSION

1. Think back to the exercise at the very beginning of this chapter. What did you see as the core of Jesus' message before reading this chapter? How did the presentation of Jesus in this chapter compare with your preexisting pictures?

2. Which aspects of Jesus' ministry are most meaningful to you?

3. The main theme of Jesus' ministry is that the Realm of God is partially present now, while God will bring it to full expression only in the future. Do you see signs of the Realm in the world today? What might you do to participate with God in manifesting signs of the Realm?

4. The Gospels present Jesus in conflict with people who do not welcome the coming of the Realm of God. Can you point to areas in which values and practices today conflict with those of the Realm of God?

CHAPTER 5

The Early Church before Paul

The ministry of Jesus is the foundation of the early church. After the resurrection and ascension, Jesus' followers continued to gather and to engage in mission. What did they believe? What did they do? We face a problem when we try to answer these questions. The book of Acts is the only document in the New Testament that describes the period of time from the resurrection to the beginning of the ministry of Paul. Acts was written by Luke (the same person who wrote the Gospel of Luke). Scholars today believe that Luke told the story of Acts from his own perspective while making use of preexisting traditions.

An apt analogy to the problem of the book of Acts is a family reunion. A group of older family members are sitting in cane-bottom rocking chairs remembering a major family event of their youth. Each senior tells the story a little differently. No one has photographs of the family event, and even if the family possessed a photographic record, the old-timers might disagree on how to interpret the visual evidence. The book of Acts is a collection of such memories of days gone by, all recast with Luke's own concerns.

In what follows, I draw on the book of Acts as well as from other inferences in the New Testament and from scholarly consensus. In this chapter, I describe the mission that Jesus set out for his followers, their existence within Judaism, their message, Pentecost, and aspects of their common life.

The Twelve Apostles: Core Leaders

Jesus had a large group of followers, but like other teachers of antiquity, he developed a group of close associates. Twelve in number, these associates were often called the "apostles" or "the disciples." Luke favors the designation "apostle," which refers to someone who is sent with a charge and who has the power to fulfill that charge.[1] These twelve became the core leadership of the new community.

The number twelve was a traditional symbol in Israel for community as God intended. The twelve apostles symbolize the reconstitution of community in the new world.

Like followers of other teachers at that time, the twelve were to learn the ways of their master, to continue his teaching after his death, to apply his teaching in fresh situations, and to engage in the mission that their teacher gave them. According to the Gospels, Jesus not only explained the Realm to the apostles but also invested them with the power to work miracles, thereby extending the ministry of Jesus in every way — preaching, teaching, and working miracles.

Jesus also taught the twelve and the wider body of his followers that they would suffer as he did. "If any want to become my followers, let them deny themselves and take up their cross and follow me" (Mark 8:34). This statement does not urge Jesus' disciples to have a suffering neurosis. It is a pastoral warning that some people in the world (such as the Roman government) will not understand the Realm of God and will resist it. In so doing, they will punish and cause suffering for its representatives.

Although Jesus had some contact with gentiles during his ministry, his focus was on announcing the presence and coming of the Realm of God in Jewish settings. Paul, Matthew, Mark, and Luke all portray Jesus instructing his followers to carry the message of the

1. In the New Testament, the term "disciples" can be confusing because it sometimes refers to the twelve but often to much larger groups of Jesus' followers. In the book of Acts, Luke usually uses "the disciples" to refer to the larger group and "the apostles" to refer to the smaller group of twelve.

Box 10. Names of the Twelve Apostles

The number of apostles is always twelve, but the names vary a little bit from list to list.

Mark 3:13-19 records:

Simon Peter (Cephas)

James the son of Zebedee

John the brother of James (James and John were sometimes called "Sons of Thunder")

Andrew

Philip

Bartholomew

Matthew

Thomas

James the son of Alphaeus

Thaddaeus

Simon the Cananean

Judas Iscariot (one of the original twelve; according to Luke, after Judas betrayed Jesus and took his own life, he was replaced by Matthias, Acts 1:12-26)

For other lists of the twelve, see Matthew 10:1-4; Luke 6:12-16; Acts 1:12-26.

Paul also referred to himself as an apostle, but he does not include himself among the twelve (for example, Romans 1:1; 1 Corinthians 1:1; 2 Corinthians 1:1; Galatians 1:1; 1 Thessalonians 2:7).

Realm of God to gentiles (Mattnew 28:16-20; Mark 13:10; Luke 24:46-49). The mission to the gentiles became a distinctive focus of the early church.

Box 11. Examples of Suffering among the Early Followers of Jesus

Jesus was crucified. The book of Acts frequently depicts the apostles and other members of the community facing resistance. In Acts, Jesus' followers are imprisoned three times (Acts 5:17-21; 12:6-11; 16:23-29). A follower of Jesus named Stephen was stoned to death (Acts 7:54–8:2), and Herod killed James with a sword (Acts 12:1-5). The book of Acts (see, for example, Acts 20:25; 28:18) implies that Paul was also martyred. Traditions not found in the New Testament recount the martyrdom of Peter.

The Followers of Jesus in Jerusalem: A Group within Judaism

After the resurrection and ascension, a group of Jesus' closest followers remained in and around Jerusalem. Some scholars think that that group of early followers of Jesus was already a new religion that had rejected Judaism. However, it is clear that the first generation of Jesus' followers thought of themselves as a community within Judaism.

- They were all Jewish.
- Their sacred scriptures were the sacred scriptures of Judaism.
- They worshiped at the temple and in synagogues.
- They practiced circumcision.
- They followed Jewish dietary customs.
- They prayed in Jewish fashion.
- They joined many other Jewish people in believing that God would end the present world and create a new one.
- Their rite of baptism was patterned after similar Jewish water rites.

You might think of the earliest followers of Jesus relating to Judaism in a way parallel to that of a small group in a congregation (such as a

Sunday-school class or some other vital group). The group is part of the congregation, but the class also has its own leaders, its own distinctive habits, and even its own checking account and projects. The class has its own life within the larger congregation. In a similar way, the initial followers of Jesus existed within Judaism.

The Message and Mission of the Early Followers of Jesus

The message that the early followers of Jesus proclaimed was quite similar to that of Jesus himself (see pp. 56-58). They believed that God had acted through Jesus announcing the end of the old age and inaugurating the Realm of God, and that God had started making his Realm appear through Jesus. They looked forward to the Second Coming of Jesus, when God would finally and fully bring the Realm into complete existence.

The mission of Jesus was the model for the mission of the earliest community. Their work was to announce the coming of this Realm, to invite people to prepare for it by repentance and baptism, and to live in the present as if the Realm of God were already dawning. They formed communities that taught about the Realm of God, and, according to the book of Acts, the apostles and others in the earliest groups of Jesus' followers performed miracles.

Jewish people who joined the Jesus movement did not convert from one religion (Judaism) to another (Christianity) but saw themselves identifying with a particular movement within Judaism. Most scholars think that the disciples of Jesus in these early years differed from other Jewish groups mainly with respect to their belief that the Realm of God had begun in the life and ministry of Jesus. Whereas many Jewish people thought that the Realm of God would come fairly soon, the followers of Jesus believed that the Realm was already upon them, and had already begun. Furthermore, the disciples of Jesus believed that Jesus himself

The disciples of Jesus believed that Jesus himself was God's special representative in announcing and initiating the Realm of God.

71

was God's special representative in announcing and initiating the Realm of God.

The Jewish people who believed in Jesus did not leave their synagogues, stop worshiping at the temple, or cease other Jewish practices. They simply believed that God had acted through Jesus and, more importantly, was about to act again through the Second Coming.

A mission to non-Jews, to gentiles, began during this time. A vital community of Jesus' followers who welcomed gentiles quickly sprang up in Antioch. Many of the first gentile converts came from the God-fearers. We saw in Chapter 2 that the "God-fearers" revered ("feared") God. God-fearers attended the synagogue and lived according to the ethical precepts of Judaism. However, they did not fully convert, perhaps because they were uneasy about circumcision or did not want to follow Jewish patterns of diet. Some of Jesus' followers likely believed that since the time was so short before the return of Jesus and the appearance in full of the Realm of God, there was no reason for the God-fearers to convert fully to Judaism. By turning away from idols (repenting) and recognizing Jesus as God's agent, gentiles could become full participants in the community of Jesus' followers. Paul joined this mission in the early 30s C.E.

The Holy Spirit Energized the Mission

In Chapter 3, we noted that the experience of the Holy Spirit was formative for the earliest followers of Jesus. The New Testament follows the Old Testament in describing the Holy Spirit as one of God's closest representatives (for example, Acts 2:1-4; Romans 8:26-27). The early communities of Jesus' followers believed that God sent the Holy Spirit to empower them for mission. The Spirit filled the believers with a profound — sometimes ecstatic — feeling of God's presence. This activity of the Spirit was a sign that the Realm of God was upon them.

While all of the books in the New Testament assume that the followers of Jesus had a special measure of the Holy Spirit, only two books describe the coming of the Spirit. In the Gospel of John, the risen Jesus "breathed on them and said, 'Receive the Holy Spirit'" (John 20:22). The book of Acts gives the longer and better-known description of the coming of the Spirit on Pentecost. The Jewish people had a harvest festival called Pentecost. The book of Acts taps into this harvest theme by suggesting that the ministries of Jesus and the early church reveal that God was harvesting history, so to speak, to bring about the Realm of God.

Prior to Pentecost, the members of the early community were together in Jerusalem but did not have a sense of mission. God sent the Holy Spirit upon them like the coming of a mighty wind (Acts 2:1-13). The Spirit filled them, caused them to speak and understand other languages, and propelled them into mission.[2] Immediately Peter preached a mighty sermon in which he stated what people needed to do to become a part of the coming Realm of God: repent, be baptized, and receive the Holy Spirit (Acts 2:38). The book of Acts repeatedly says that the Holy Spirit led Jesus' followers in witness, sustained them in times of difficulty, and prompted them to live for the Second Coming.

The Life of the Early Community

Most scholars think that the early Jerusalem community worshiped in the temple and in synagogues on Friday night and Saturday (the

---

2. In Acts 2:1-13, the Holy Spirit caused the believers to speak and hear in recognized languages other than their native languages. Pentecost is thus a day of mutual understanding. It contrasts with the story of the building of the tower of Babel in Genesis 11 in which people wrongly sought to build a tower to heaven. Prior to working on the tower, all human beings spoke the same language. But when God thwarted their plans, God also gave them many different languages so that they could not easily understand one another. Thus, they could not try to rebuild the tower. In 1 Corinthians 12-14, the apostle Paul speaks about another kind of spiritually empowered language. In 1 Corinthians, the people "speak in tongues" (sometimes called "unknown tongues" or "glossolalia," which is simply Greek for "speaking in tongues"). The latter phenomenon consists of syllables that are strung together but that do not come from a known language.

usual Jewish times of worship), and gathered again either Sunday morning or Sunday evening. Sunday was the day on which God raised Jesus from the dead. Moreover, as the first day of the week, Sunday represented the coming of the new world. Worship at the temple or synagogue thus expressed their continuity with Judaism. Worship on Sunday represented their confidence that the resurrection of Jesus pointed to the coming of the Realm of God.

Worship services often took place in homes that were large enough to have a meeting area where the community would worship and share a meal where rich and poor alike would eat together and no one would be in want. Scholars think that the services of worship were similar to those in the synagogue, beginning with a call to worship (perhaps from a psalm), and including singing, readings from the Bible (the Old Testament), a sermon, and prayer.

In addition, many services were marked by the congregation eating from a common loaf of bread and drinking from a cup of wine. In the New Testament, this meal is sometimes called the breaking of bread (in Acts), the Lord's Supper (1 Corinthians 11:20), or the marriage feast of the lamb (Revelation 19:9).[3] Jesus began this traditional meal on the night before he was arrested.

Jewish people at that time expected that after God had brought about his Realm, God would put on a great banquet to celebrate the new reality. The last supper that Jesus ate with his closest followers anticipated this last great banquet. Note that in Mark, after drinking from the cup, Jesus says, "'Truly I tell you, I will never again drink of the fruit of the vine until that day when I drink it new in the kingdom [Realm] of God'" (Mark 14:25). After the resurrection, Jesus' followers understood the meal in the

Jesus' followers understood the meal in the same way — as celebrating in the present in anticipation of the great banquet at the end of time.

---

3. In today's church, this sacred meal is sometimes called the Eucharist. This title is from the Greek verb for "I give thanks" *(eucharisteō),* which is used in most accounts of the supper in the New Testament. However, the New Testament does not specifically use the word "Eucharist" as a name for the sacred meal.

Box 12. The Last Supper in the New Testament

The last supper is described in Matthew 26:26-30; Mark 14:22-26; and Luke 22:17-20. Paul speaks of this supper in 1 Corinthians 11:23-25. The last supper in the New Testament is a model for the Lord's Supper observed in many churches today. The heart of the Lord's Supper is "the words of institution," derived from these narratives. The wording varies a little bit from writer to writer. Paul's version is widely used. "The Lord Jesus on the night when he was betrayed took a loaf of bread, and when he had given thanks, he broke it and said, 'This is my body that is broken for you. Do this in remembrance of me.' In the same way he took a cup also, after supper, saying, 'This cup is the new covenant in my blood. Do this, as often as you drink it, in remembrance of me'" (1 Corinthians 11:23-25).

---

same way — as celebrating in the present in anticipation of the great banquet at the end of time.

The followers of Jesus also baptized persons joining the community. The Jewish people already washed in water as a part of their ritual cleansing. They also immersed gentiles in water when they converted to Judaism. John the Baptist immersed (baptized) people in preparation for the end of the world and the coming Realm of God. The baptismal rite (immersion) practiced by the earliest followers of Jesus was similar to John's baptismal rite except that it took place in the name of Jesus himself, that is, acknowledging that Jesus is the one through whom God is bringing his Realm.[4]

The community had little formal structure but depended largely upon the charismatic leadership of the apostles. However, the congregation created leadership positions in response to practi-

---

4. In the New Testament period, the followers of Jesus had two traditions for baptizing. In the book of Acts, baptism takes place in the name of Jesus only. In the church to which Matthew wrote, baptism took place in the name of "the Father, and of the Son, and of the Holy Spirit" (Matthew 28:19). Today, most churches follow Matthew's custom, but a few churches baptize in the name of Jesus only.

cal needs and the leading of the Spirit. For instance, when a dispute broke out because the Greek-speaking widows did not receive as much food in the daily distribution of charitable support as Hebrew-speaking widows, the community created the office of "deacon" and authorized the deacons through the laying on of hands (Acts 6:1-6). The work of the first deacons was to ensure the fair distribution of food.

"They Had All Things in Common"

Today's readers are often fascinated by the brief account of the early community in the book of Acts. "They devoted themselves to the apostles' teaching and fellowship, to the breaking of bread and the prayers" (Acts 2:42). The apostles' teaching, of course, is the teaching about the coming of the Realm of God. The term "fellowship" refers not only to close relationships but to entering into a partnership with one another to carry out the common mission. The phrase "breaking of bread" refers to the breaking of bread and pouring out of wine, or the Lord's Supper (see p. 75). The prayers were similar to Jewish prayers looking forward to the coming of the Realm of God.

The book of Acts also notes that "awe came upon everyone, because many wonders and signs were being done by the apostles." These followers continued to perform miracles following the pattern of Jesus (Acts 2:43).

Luke further observes, "All who believed were together and had all things in common; they would sell their possessions and goods and distribute the proceeds to all, as any had need" (Acts 2:44-45). Why did the members of the community share their material resources? Because in the Realm of God, all are to be provided for abundantly. Sharing of possessions was the way God provided for all who had need. This memory is Luke's idealized presentation of how Christian communities should be. To be truthful, we do not know whether the earliest followers of Jesus actually held all things in common in the way described in this passage. Luke uses this picture to spur his readers toward greater sharing.

Box 13. Common Ownership

Luke expands on the theme of sharing of possessions. "Now the whole group of those who believed were of one heart and soul, and no one claimed private ownership of any possessions, but everything they owned was held in common. . . . There was not a needy person among them, for as many as owned lands or houses sold them and brought the proceeds of what was sold. They laid it at the apostles' feet, and it was distributed to each as any had need" (Acts 4:32-35).

Jesus' Followers Were Soon Called the "Church," and Later "Christians"

We do not know who first used the name "church" for Jesus' followers or when they did so. The word "church" in the original Greek in which the New Testament was written simply means "called out." In Greek society the word "church" referred to an assembly of free people who were called to discuss civic affairs. But the Old Testament provides a better understanding. This testament was originally written in Hebrew. When the Old Testament books were translated into Greek, the translators used the word "church" to translate the Hebrew word for "congregation" or "assembly" (for example, in Deuteronomy 31:30 Moses recites his final song in the hearing of "the whole assembly of Israel"). The Old Testament writers understood that God called Israel from the other nations to be a conduit through which God would bless all peoples. The designation "church," for the early Christian community, identifies them as being in the tradition of Judaism.

The situation is murkier with respect to the name "Christian." A Christian, of course, is one who follows Christ. Although we today often refer to the earliest followers of Jesus as "Christians," that name occurs in the New Testament only three times (Acts 11:26; 26:28; 1 Peter 4:16). We do not know how it originated. Acts declares simply, "And it was in Antioch that the disciples were first called 'Christians'" (Acts 11:26). The name may have been given to the disciples by outsiders as a way of identifying the followers of Jesus as a particular group within the Jewish community. Some scholars think the term "Christian" may first have had negative connotations, much like referring to a person today as a member of the Ku Klux Klan. The early Christians were newcomers and strange. The term would have been a way to point them out and isolate them. Only later, according to this theory, did Christians claim this term as a positive way of naming people who follow Christ.

QUESTIONS FOR DISCUSSION

1. If you are a member of a church or other faith community, compare and contrast the understanding of the message and mission of the early church with your own.

2. Think about how the worship of the first generation of Jesus' followers is similar or dissimilar to your own.

3. The early church community was loosely organized and adapted quickly to its changing needs. How does that compare to the organization of your own group?

4. According to the book of Acts, Jesus' earliest followers "had all things in common." From that common body, they provided material resources for all in the community. How do you respond to that idea today? What can you and your community do to see that there is "not a needy person among them"?

CHAPTER 6

Paul: Apostle to the Gentiles

I often tell my classes at the seminary where I serve: "The apostle Paul is the reason you and I serve the living God and not idols." My students are almost entirely "gentiles" or non-Jews. Paul was the primary apostle, or missionary, to the gentiles. Idolatry was one of the quintessential marks of gentile life in Paul's day. Without Paul, I might well be an idolater, serving dead idols rather than the living God of Israel.

In this chapter, I summarize Paul's story based largely on his own writings. For reasons stated below, I also compare and contrast Paul's own remarks with the picture of Paul in the book of Acts. We begin with what we know about Paul's early life, and then focus on his call as "apostle to the gentiles." The latter part of the chapter summarizes both the reasons why Paul wrote the seven letters and the content of those letters.

To construct our understanding of Paul the apostle, we have very little literature to draw upon, and that literature is spread over a good many years.

Paul became a follower of Jesus about 33-35 C.E., wrote 1 Thessalonians, the first of his surviving letters, around 49 C.E., wrote the book of Romans around 58 C.E., and was executed around 62-64 C.E. Thus, to construct our understanding of Paul the apostle, we have very little literature to draw upon, and that literature is spread over a good many years.

Two Pictures of Paul in the New Testament

The New Testament contains two pictures of Paul. (1) The seven letters that Paul actually wrote are the main source of our knowledge of Paul.[1] While these letters open wide windows into Paul's thought, they do not really give us a lot of information about Paul's life. (2) Our other source is the book of Acts, more than half of which focuses on Paul. The book of Acts, of course, was written by Luke, and most scholars today think that Luke told the story of Paul not to provide a documentary of Paul's life but to interpret Paul in such a way as to serve Luke's own purposes. Ironically, the narrative of Paul in Acts is so vivid that it is more familiar to many people than Paul's own writings.

Both Paul's own writings and the book of Acts agree that Paul was called to be a missionary to the gentiles. Paul names himself an apostle (missionary), whereas the book of Acts almost never uses that title. The book of Acts and the letter to the Galatians give slightly different versions of the outcome of the Jerusalem Council (Acts 15:1-35; Galatians 2:1-10). This council was a meeting convened to deal with the conversion of the gentiles who followed Jesus but had not completely converted to Judaism. In Acts, Paul is a great speaker, whereas Paul reports that some Corinthians said, "His letters are weighty and strong, but his bodily presence is weak, and his speech contemptible" (2 Corinthians 10:10). In Acts, Paul works miracles, whereas Paul never refers to such activity. The book of Acts never mentions that Paul wrote letters, whereas his letters are the only material that we have from Paul's own hand. In Acts, Paul makes three clearly defined missionary journeys, and makes a fourth journey under guard to Rome, whereas the historical Paul does not provide such detailed accounts.

These two pictures are not so much in direct conflict as they offer different perspectives. When in doubt, the reader should follow the historical Paul. But we should be familiar with the picture of

---

1. These letters are 1 Thessalonians, 1 and 2 Corinthians, Galatians, Philippians, Philemon, and Romans.

Paul in Acts and respect Luke's use of it to address situations in Luke's own community.

Paul's Background: Persecutor

Paul says little about his early life and background. In Philippians, he does say that he was "circumcised on the eighth day, a member of the people of Israel, of the tribe of Benjamin, a Hebrew born of Hebrews; as to the law, a Pharisee; . . . as to righteousness under the law, blameless" (Philippians 3:5-6). This description means that Paul was highly respected within Judaism. Note, please, that Paul does not ever criticize Judaism as such. The book of Acts records that Paul had been a student of Rabbi Gamaliel, an important teacher in Judaism (Acts 5:34-39; 22:3). Being a student of Gamaliel would have given Paul a social standing similar to the standing that accompanies attending an Ivy League university today.

Both Paul and Luke agree that a young and zealous Paul persecuted the church (Galatians 1:13). What did it mean to persecute the church? The Roman Empire did not allow people in antiquity to carry out random acts of violence on one another, but the empire did authorize the synagogues to use controlled methods to discipline their own members who had become unfaithful. The synagogue could even lash a person up to thirty-nine times (note 2 Corinthians 11:24). The purpose of such discipline was to awaken unfaithful Jewish people and to encourage them to return to faithfully following the Jewish faith. Paul was not a vigilante but was authorized to bring Jewish followers of Jesus to the synagogue for discipline.

Being a student of Gamaliel would have given Paul a social standing similar to the standing that accompanies attending an Ivy League university today.

People were not likely disciplined for believing that Jesus was God's agent in the coming of the Realm of God. Many other Jewish groups put forward their own candidates for Messiah without reprimand. The most likely reason the early Christians faced sanction was that some of Jesus' followers were already welcoming gentiles without asking them to convert fully to Judaism. A traditional synagogue would regard such behavior as a violation of Jewish identity.

Paul: Apostle to the Gentiles

According to Galatians, God called Paul to be an apostle to the gentiles. Paul says plainly that God "set me apart before I was born" and "called me through [divine] grace . . . to reveal his Son to me, *so that I might proclaim him among the Gentiles*" (Galatians 1:15-16).[2] According to many Jewish writers, God would reunite the Jewish and gentile communities in the Realm.

Box 14. Saul and Paul: Two Names for the Same Person

In his own letters, Paul refers to himself only by the name "Paul." In the book of Acts, Paul is initially called "Saul" and only later "Paul." I grew up thinking that the change in name represented Paul's change in life: from "Saul," persecutor of the church, to "Paul," apostle for Jesus. However, "Saul" is simply the Hebrew form of "Paul." When Paul embarks upon the gentile mission, the book of Acts uses the name "Paul" because it would have been more familiar to audiences outside of Palestine (especially gentiles) than "Saul."

Note that Paul does not say that he was converted from one religion to another. Rather, he believed that the God of Israel called him from one mode of serving God to another. The gentiles to whom Paul preached, by contrast, did convert from one religion to another — from worshiping dead idols to loving and serving the living God of Israel (for example, 1 Thessalonians 1:9-10; 4:5). Some Jewish

---

2. The book of Acts also mentions Paul being called to be a missionary to the gentiles (Acts 9:15; 22:14-15; 26:16-18).

people did come into Paul's congregations because they believed that the ministry of Jesus was that definitive sign that God was about to end this age and begin the age of the Realm, but there is no indication that they ceased following the ways of Judaism.[3]

For Paul, the coming of the Realm of God will fulfill the promise that God made to Sarah and Abraham to bless both the Jewish and gentile communities (Romans 4:16-25). From this point of view, the gentile mission was not an innovation in Judaism. It was not a departure from the Old Testament. From Paul's perspective, the gentile mission was the last stage in Israel's mission in the world.

A close reading of Paul's own letters shows that Paul did not counsel the gentile converts to avoid Judaism. Just the opposite: The apostle encourages the gentiles not only to abandon idols but to adopt key Jewish perspectives on life. The gentiles were to believe that the God of the Old Testament is the only true and living God, and they were to live in ways that respected and supported one another. Though Paul does not often use the word "covenant," he sought for the gentile congregations to live in covenant with one another. He wanted the gentiles and Jews to share the most sacred bond, living in the coming Reign of God. Paul thus hoped to "judaize" the gentiles, that is, he encouraged them to live in the spirit of Judaism even though they did not convert fully to Judaism.

The Coming Realm of God:
The Center of Paul's Message

Paul did not write much about the life and teaching of Jesus. In fact, Paul directly quotes Jesus on only one occasion.[4] Paul does speak

---

3. As we note in Chapter 3, both Paul (Galatians 2:1-10) and the book of Acts (Acts 15:1-35) report that conflict developed between Paul and some in the congregation in Jerusalem regarding the gentile mission. The Jerusalem Conference forged a workable way forward, though its outcome is described a little differently by Paul and by Acts.

4. In the midst of calling the Corinthian congregation to respect one another when they meet together to partake of the Lord's Supper, Paul cites these two sen-

generally about the significance of Jesus' earthly life by citing a hymn sung in the early church saying that Jesus existed with God before Jesus was born into this earthly life. "Christ," in this passage, refers to the preexistent Jesus. It is one of the titles for Jesus in the New Testament that meant "anointed one," or chosen for his task. So, the passage goes, Christ "emptied himself, taking the form of a slave" who was born as a human being and who was put to death (Philippians 2:6-8).

For Paul, the significance of Jesus comes into focus with the death and resurrection. As one of my teachers put it, "For Paul the death and resurrection of Jesus mark the turning point of the ages." While the rulers of the old age put Christ to death, God demonstrated the coming Realm by raising Jesus from the dead. Indeed, the new world is the ultimate goal of God's work. The resurrection of Christ is the "first fruits" of the coming age, again using a harvest metaphor; the resurrection is the beginning, but the full harvest and benefit is coming soon after. Paul expects

"For Paul the death and resurrection of Jesus mark the turning point of the ages."

the end of the present world to come "when he [Christ] returns and gives the kingdom [or all earthly rule] to God the Father, after he has destroyed every ruler and every authority and power" (paraphrase of 1 Corinthians 15:24).

Paul saw the congregations he founded as continuing this witness. They were to invite other gentiles to come to the God of Israel. Since the congregations had already begun to experience aspects of the future Realm of God in the midst of their present, they were to live in community in ways that embodied the coming Realm.

As we will see more fully in the next chapter, Paul wrote the letters that we have in the New Testament because things happened in the congregations that violated the spirit of the Realm of God. The congregations were no longer living as enclaves of the future in the

---

tences of Jesus: "This is my body that is for you. Do this in remembrance of me," and "This cup is the new covenant in my blood. Do this, as often as you drink it, in remembrance of me" (1 Corinthians 11:24-25).

present but were living according to the values and behaviors of the old age. Paul wrote to help them recover their lost life.

Paul's Missionary Activity

Paul wrote letters to congregations to deal with problems in the life of the community. This apostle did not write an autobiography, so we do not have a nifty self-portrait. Based on the autobiographical remarks that Paul makes in his letters and on our knowledge of ancient missionary practices, we can reconstruct a general picture of Paul's missionary life.

In both his letters and the book of Acts Paul reports that he worked a trade and that he supported himself by the work of his own hands. He did not live off the gifts of the people whom he served. Paul says that he supported himself so that he would not be beholden to people to whom he needed to say a firm and critical word (1 Thessalonians 2:1-12). He himself does not identify his trade.

The book of Acts describes Paul as a tentmaker (Acts 18:3). Tents were usually made of leather or of woven animal hair, and tentmakers typically had a small booth in a public marketplace where they worked with hand tools to make tents.

Paul likely established congregations as an outgrowth of his work. In those days, teachers and philosophers often had such a

---

Box 15. References to Paul Working with His Own Hands

In the following passages from Paul's own letters, the apostle refers to working with his hands: 1 Corinthians 4:12; 9:6; 2 Corinthians 11:27; and 1 Thessalonians 2:9, where Paul says, "You remember our labor and toil, brothers and sisters; we worked night and day, so that we might not burden any of you while we proclaimed to you the gospel of God."

trade, so that people would come to the marketplace to engage in philosophical and religious discussion with the teacher-workers.

We can imagine Paul presenting the gospel of God's coming Realm with Christ as God's agent in the marketplace. When a small community had formed, they would meet in a house for teaching, preaching, worship, the sacred meal, and fellowship. Paul would stay in a community long enough to establish at least one house-based church and would then move on to a begin a new community. The book of Acts also describes Paul visiting synagogues and presenting Jesus as the agent of God's Realm to synagogue audiences.

We can imagine Paul presenting the gospel of God's coming Realm with Christ as God's agent in the marketplace.

After Paul left, he communicated with house-churches through letters and envoys. A congregation might write him describing a problem and seeking his advice, or he might receive reports from people who had recently come from a congregation. Paul replied with the letters that we now have (and perhaps others that are lost).

The book of Acts offers a fuller chronology of Paul's ministry, though we cannot be certain to what degree Acts gives us a reliable picture. After his divine call, Paul preached in Damascus, visited Jerusalem, and worked in Tarsus and Antioch (Acts 9:1-30; 11:25-30). The book of Acts then narrates three famous missionary journeys, each one taking Paul further and further toward the west: (1) Acts 13:1-14:28; (2) Acts 15:40-18:22; (3) Acts 18:23-20:38. Paul journeyed to Jerusalem in Acts 21:1-16. These journeys are followed by an extensive narrative of Paul's journey to Rome (Acts 21:17-28:31). For Paul's missionary journeys, see the map on p. 89.

The End of Paul's Life in Rome

Naturally, Paul does not record the end of his own life. He does mention that he was imprisoned (2 Corinthians 11:23; Philippians 1:7, 12-14, 17; Philemon 1, 9). Traditions as early as the second century C.E. claim that the Roman government executed Paul in Rome.

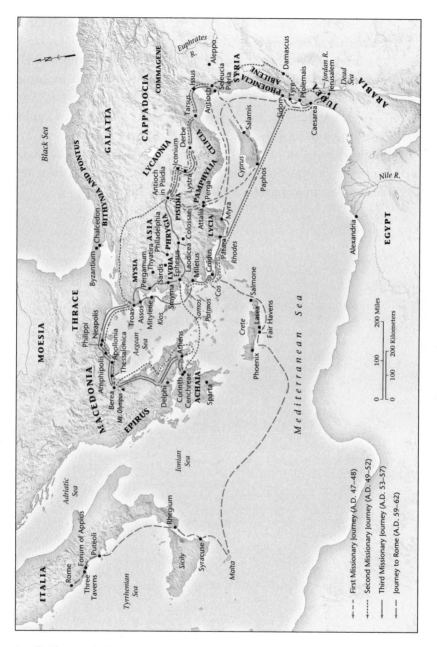

Paul's Three Missionary Journeys and Paul's Journey to Rome, according to the Book of Acts

Many scholars think that Paul was put to death as part of a persecution of Christians by Emperor Nero in the year 64 C.E.

The book of Acts does not directly state that the Romans killed Paul, but it does imply that the apostle was martyred while in Rome (Acts 9:16; 19:21; 20:22-25; 21:10-14; 23:11; 26:32; 27:23-25). As noted above, much of the book of Acts focuses on the end of Paul's life, including a description of his arrest in Jerusalem (Acts 21:27-36), his journey to Rome, with several trials along the way (Acts 21:37–28:16), a shipwreck (Acts 27:9–28:10), and his final days under house arrest in Rome (Acts 28:16-31).

QUESTIONS FOR DISCUSSION

1. Before reading this chapter, did you have images of Paul in your mind? Did you have feelings or impressions of this apostle? If so, what were they?

2. Can you tell if your earlier thoughts about Paul were more influenced by the picture of Paul in the book of Acts or by Paul's own writings?

3. The center of Paul's invitation to gentiles was to turn from the idols of the Greeks and Romans and to embrace the living God made known to them through Jesus Christ in order to become a part of the coming Realm of God. Do you think this invitation is still valid for today? If so, what idols do you see people following today?

4. Paul changed his mind. Before his call to be apostle to the gentiles, he believed that he served God by persecuting Jesus' followers. After his call, he concluded that his earlier attitude was wrong and that he should serve God by engaging in the very mission in which he had earlier persecuted followers of Christ. Have you had such changes of perspective in your own life?

5. Paul spent much of his life as a missionary to the gentiles. God may not call you to leave your home and travel as Paul did, but if you are a believer, in what situations in your own world can you make a witness that is similar to Paul's?

6. A document from the second century c.e. called "The Acts of Paul and Thecla" contains a description of the person of Paul. The unknown writer says that Paul was "a man of small stature, with a bald head and crooked legs, in a good state of body, with eyebrows meeting and nose somewhat hooked, full of friendliness."* We do not know whether this description contains an actual remi-

---

* "The Acts of Paul," 3, trans. R. McL. Wilson, in Edgar Hennecke, *New Testament Apocrypha,* ed. Wilhelm Schneemelcher (Philadelphia: Westminster, 1964), p. 354. This document tells the story of an encounter between Paul and a woman named Thecla. The encounter reflects favorably on Thecla as a woman authorized to preach and baptize.

niscence of Paul's appearance. But the existence of this portrait raises a question. Would it make any difference to you to have physical descriptions for people from the New Testament?

7. As you go from this chapter into the letters discussed in the next one, what do you still want to know about Paul? If you could ask Paul a question, what would it be?

CHAPTER 7

The Letters of Paul

Today we usually write letters, or send e-mails, for one of two reasons. (1) We may receive a message from someone to which we need to respond. Or (2) we may initiate a contact with someone. We may ask a question or make a request or let them know about something to which we hope they will give attention.

Paul's letters tend to be of the first type. He received a communication from a congregation — a letter or a report from someone who had recently been in the congregation. The letter or the report informed Paul about something happening in the congregation that the apostle needed to address. So he wrote a letter to encourage a change of thinking and behavior in the congregation.

Paul's letters were only half of a two-way conversation. You have probably been in a situation in which you were intentionally or unintentionally listening to one side of a phone call. You hear what one party is saying, but to get the full gist of the conversation, you need the other side.

Fortunately, Paul left some clues in his letters that help us reconstruct the other side of the conversations. Some of these clues are direct, as when he says, "Concerning the things about which you wrote." Other clues are indirect.

In this chapter, I first review how people wrote letters in antiquity. I then go through the seven authentic letters of Paul, recalling both the situation in the congregation that prompted Paul to write, and Paul's response.

The Form of Letters in the Ancient World

In antiquity letters were written in a fairly uniform style. Paul's letters follow the protocol of other letters in antiquity. Each part of the letter has a different function. When you read a letter, it helps you understand how each part functions. By way of analogy, when I take my car to a mechanic, I have different concerns when I am looking at the motor, the interior, the body, the tires, the insurance policy, or the amount of money I owe on the car. In a similar way, as an interpreter I listen for different things when looking at each of the parts that make up the letter.

1. **Opening formula**
   From the writer (Paul)
   To the recipients (the church at Corinth . . . or elsewhere)
   Greeting ("Grace to you and peace . . .")

2. **Thanksgiving**
   This section both gives thanks to God for the relationship between Paul and the recipients and reveals the main theme of the letter.

3. **Main body of the letter**
   Paul sets out the circumstances that called for the letter (how the community has violated the Realm of God) and gives the writer's guidance for the future (how the people can make appropriate changes).

4. **Call to right behavior (exhortation)**
   Paul urges the recipients to live in ways that are consistent with the Realm of God.

5. **Closing formula**
   Benediction or blessing ("The grace of Jesus Christ be with you. . . .")
   Occasional reference to scribes, the envoy carrying the letter, and so on.

94

The letters in the New Testament do not always conform in a pure way to this outline. The letter writers mix the various elements, especially the main body and the call to right behavior. Occasionally letters omit particular elements. For example, Galatians does not have a thanksgiving.

Box 16. Chart Showing the Parts of Paul's Letters

	Rom	1 Cor	2 Cor	Gal	Phil	1 Thess	Philem
Opening	1:1-7	1:1-3	1:1-2	1:1-5	1:1-2	1:1	vv. 1-3
Thanksgiving	1:8-17	1:4-9	1:3-7		1:3-11	1:2-3:13	vv. 4-11
Body	1:18-11:36	1:10-4:21	1:8-7:16	1:6-5:12	1:12-2:30	4:1-5:11	vv. 12-21
Call to Action	12:1-15:33	5:1-15:58	8:1-13:10	5:13-6:10	3:1-4:20	5:12-25	v. 22
Closing	16:1-27	16:1-24	13:11-13	6:11-18	4:21-22	5:26-28	vv. 23-25

1 and 2 Corinthians do not strictly conform to the letter form, perhaps because the material in these letters may originally have been scattered in four (or more) letters that have now been combined into two.

Galatians has no thanksgiving paragraph, perhaps because Paul was so eager to get to the body of the letter.

1 Thessalonians is unusual in that the thanksgiving comprises over half the letter.

There were two kinds of letters in antiquity — those intended to be read publicly and those meant to be read privately. Most of Paul's "epistles" or letters are public letters. Few people in the ancient world could read. Paul intended that a literate member of the congregation read his letters aloud. The congregation would receive the letter in much the same way that people listen to a sermon today.

Some Common Themes

While each letter deals with particular questions and issues, some of the same concerns come up in multiple letters. In nearly every case, members of the congregation were not living in ways consistent with the Realm of God. These common issues include:

- Whether the congregation was faithful to the teachings of Paul, or deviated toward the messages of lesser teachers who had visited the communities.
- The degree to which the community was living in ways that both embodied and prepared them for the Realm and the Second Coming of Jesus.
- The relationship of Jewish and gentile peoples, both in the church and in larger life settings.
- The degree to which the behavior of some members was destroying the sense of community and mutual commitment in the congregation.
- Sexual behavior.

When you read each letter, you need to pay attention to the particular details of these concerns in the congregation to whom the letter was written.

1 Thessalonians

1 Thessalonians is unusual in that Paul devotes more than half of the letter to the thanksgiving section (1 Thessalonians 1:2–3:13). This long section shows the apostle's overflowing love for the community. After Paul had established the congregation, he left them, but he longed to know how they were doing and so sent Timothy to visit (1 Thessalonians 2:17–3:5). The report that Timothy brought back to Paul encouraged the apostle at a time when he was in distress (1 Thessalonians 3:6-13).

The Thessalonian congregation was made up of gentiles who

had converted from Roman and Greek gods to the God of Israel. When doing so, they left behind the lax sexual morality typical of gentile culture and adopted the more restrained sexual practices of the Jewish people. Their unconverted neighbors harassed them because of this and other behavior. In Paul's absence, members of the congregation were tempted to return to their former practices.

In the body of the letter, Paul encourages the Thessalonian congregation to continue to refrain from sexual immorality, to love one another, and to live quietly so as not to disturb the peace (1 Thessalonians 4:1-12). The unconverted friends and neighbors of the Thessalonian Christians may have responded with hostility, especially since the converted gentiles followed the strict moral and sexual codes of the Jewish people. Paul urges the Thessalonians to continue to refrain from fornication (having sex outside of marriage) and other aberrations in relationships and to continue to adhere to other things Paul had taught.

Paul assures the Thessalonian church that when Jesus comes, all of those who have died will be gathered with him in the Realm of God.

The major issue within the congregation that Paul addresses comes to light in 1 Thessalonians 4:13–5:11. Some people in the community had questions about the resurrection. Some members of the congregation had died, and those left behind wondered what would happen to the deceased at the time of the Second Coming. Paul assures the Thessalonian church that when Jesus comes, all of those who have died will be gathered with him in the Realm of God.

Galatians

Galatians is one of the most difficult letters for readers to interpret. When we read Galatians naively, it is easy to get the impression that Paul rejects Judaism, declares it an obsolete religion, and believes that Christianity has replaced Judaism. It sounds like Christ freed gentiles from legalistic obedience to the law. This way of thinking about Galatians has been quite popular and is even preached today.

97

However, a closer look reveals that this point of view is at odds with Paul and Judaism that we saw in the previous chapter.

In the last twenty years, many scholars have found a better interpretation of Galatians that is consistent with the picture we have of Paul in the rest of the New Testament, as discussed in Chapter 6. According to this interpretation, after Paul established the congregation in Galatia and had moved on, some visitors came into the community and preached another version of the gospel. These visitors were gentiles who had converted to Judaism as adults and *who did not understand the law* (Torah). They thought that obedience to the law functioned as a work that earned God's love. According to their teaching, gentiles had to convert to Judaism to be included in the Realm of God, and to perform the works of the law (such as circumcision and keeping food laws) to win God's approval. They had a legalistic mind-set that regarded God as a punitive accountant. Some Galatians believed them.

Paul begins his reply by stressing that his teaching in Galatia had been directly authorized both by God and by the church in Jerusalem (Galatians 1:11–2:10). The heart of Paul's response is that the visitors have misunderstood the purpose of the law. It was never intended to prescribe works that would lead God to accept human beings. The law was intended to be a guide for Jewish people until the coming of the Realm of God. For the gentiles to adopt the false understanding of the law set out by the visitors was to take a giant religious step backward. Moreover, Paul believed that Christ would come soon. The gentiles in Galatia should concentrate on living faithfully in view of the Realm of God rather than being sidetracked by a false notion of the law.

1 and 2 Corinthians

1 and 2 Corinthians are at least two separate letters.[1] Many scholars think that the problems in Corinth resulted from outsider groups

1. Not only are 1 and 2 Corinthians currently printed as two separate letters,

visiting Corinth and teaching that the center of the gospel is the present experience of the Spirit. The intruders may have taught that there would be no end of the world, no final judgment, no resurrection of the dead or coming new world. For the visitors, those who have the Spirit are freed from traditional restraints (such as traditional Jewish sexual morality). Many issues stemmed from these outsiders' assumptions. Here are a few of the most important in the letters to the Corinthians. The congregation was badly divided. Paul encouraged the congregation to live as a genuine community of the Realm of God (1 Corinthians 1:10-17). The outsiders taught that God's power operates in a spectacular, ecstatic, showy manner. Paul reminded the congregation that the cross (and its weakness) and resurrection are the means whereby God signals the coming of the Realm (1 Corinthians 1:18-4:20).

Many in the congregation engaged in improper sexual behavior. Paul asserted that the congregation needed to correct unhealthy sexual expression to be prepared for the Realm of God (1 Corinthians 5:1-7:40). Some in the congregation ate food that had been offered to idols, as was the practice in that society. Food offered in various temples and cults would then be sold later for human consumption. Some found no problem eating such fare, but doing so offended other members. Paul agreed that those who ate the food offered to idols were free to do so but admonished them to refrain out of deference for those offended. Persisting in such a trivial choice undermined the unity of those seeking to live the unity of the Realm of God (1 Corinthians 8:1-13; 10:1-11:1). Continuing this line of thought, Paul used himself as an example: he was an apostle who had distinct rights (such as to be supported financially by the community), but he had not exercised those rights so as to be of bigger service to the community. Indeed, he supported himself while in Corinth, thus not sponging off the community (1 Corinthians 9:1-27). Some women were praying in public with heads uncovered. The apostle preferred that women pray with covered heads in keeping

---

but many scholars think that they may originally have been four (or more) letters now compressed into two documents.

with local social mores (1 Corinthians 11:2-16). When the community gathered for the Lord's Supper, they were divided along the lines of rich and poor. This was an affront to the Realm of God. Paul called the congregation to eat together in a spirit of sharing and concern for everyone's needs (1 Corinthians 11:17-34). The worship of the congregation was in chaos because some members overvalued speaking in tongues and other spectacular gifts. People were speaking in tongues and exercising other spiritual gifts inappropriately in worship. The apostle taught that all gifts are equal and that all are to be used to build up the community in worship (1 Corinthians 12:1–14:40). Some denied the Second Coming of Jesus. They felt free to do whatever they wanted. Paul returns to the core of his teaching: all will be raised (and judged) in bodily form for what they have done in their bodies (1 Corinthians 15:1-58). So-called super apostles taught that Paul's suffering showed that he was not a true apostle. From Paul's point of view, his suffering was *proof* of his faithful service. The Corinthians themselves were Paul's best letter of authentic apostleship (2 Corinthians 1:8–7:15; 10:1–12:13). The Corinthian congregation had not responded generously to the offering Paul was collecting for the poor in Jerusalem. The apostle exhorted them to do so (2 Corinthians 8:1–9:15).

In sum, Paul wrote these letters to address specific situations in the Corinthian congregation. The apostle called the Corinthians to a more authentic and engaged faith that would work against their competitive individualism and take with utmost seriousness what living in the coming Realm of God would look like in their communal life together.

Philippians

Paul was imprisoned when he wrote the letter to the Philippians. The congregation had heard of his situation and sent both prayers and material resources in support (Philippians 1:19; 4:17-18). Preachers often comment on Paul's joyful attitude in this letter. Despite the fact that he is in jail, he looks forward to the return of

Christ when he will be reunited with the Philippians and all the faithful in the Realm of God (Philippians 1:10, 28; 2:12; 3:20; 4:1).

However, some other preachers (whom Paul uncharitably calls "dogs," "evil workers," and "enemies of the cross of Christ") disturbed the congregation with their teaching that the gentile Philippians must perform certain works in order for God to save them. For example, the Philippians must be circumcised (Philippians 3:2-3). Very likely these unwelcome guests were similar to the intruders in Galatia: gentiles who had converted to Judaism and misrepresented the law.

Paul insists that those who acknowledge the work of Christ are already in the embrace of the Realm of God (Philippians 1:11; 2:6-11; 3:3, 9-11). Of course, since the Philippians are people of the Realm, they should live the Realm of God in all circumstances (Philippians 1:27; 2:1-5, 12, 15; 4:4-8).

Philemon

Paul wrote to Philemon regarding a slave (Onesimus) (pronounced "oh-NES-ee-moos") escaping from his master (Philemon) and fleeing to the imprisoned Paul. The apostle developed a strong attachment to Onesimus (Philemon 10, 12-13, 16) but believed that the slave should return to his master. Paul would like Philemon to receive the slave as a brother (v. 16). Before escaping, Onesimus had evidently done something (not specified) to wrong Philemon (v. 18). Paul wrote with great diplomacy to win Philemon's trust and approval. Scholars disagree as to whether Paul wanted Philemon to free Onesimus or whether it was enough for Philemon to welcome the slave home and not to punish the returning fugitive.

Romans

Like Galatians, the book of Romans is hard to interpret. Christians have often used it — in a manner similar to their use of Galatians —

to cast a negative verdict on Judaism and especially on the law (Torah). Interpreters of Romans in this stream often see Judaism as a religion based on works, and Jewish people as struggling under the terrible burden of the law, knowing that they can never do enough to satisfy God. Christ releases people from the chains of the law. Indeed, Christ saves people from Judaism.

A recent wave of scholarship views Romans quite differently. According to this perspective, gentile members in the congregation at Rome had developed a superior attitude toward the Jewish people and discounted the Jewish heritage.

Paul wrote Romans for the purpose of persuading the gentile members of the congregation to respect their Jewish sisters and brothers as well as the Jewish religion itself. Indeed, the gentiles needed to adopt some Jewish ways of thinking and behaving. In the climactic section of the letter, Paul exults, "Welcome one another, therefore, just as Christ has welcomed you" (Romans 15:7).

This perspective drives each section of Romans. At the beginning, Paul points out that apart from God's work in Christ, the gentiles were hopelessly doomed to condemnation (Romans 1:18-32). Through Christ, God welcomed gentiles into God's Realm even as God welcomed the Jewish people (Romans 2:1–3:31). Such a reunion had been God's plan since Sarah and Abraham (Romans 4:1-25). One of the goals of the ministry of Christ is welcoming gentiles into the Realm of God (Romans 5:1-21). Baptism is the means whereby gentiles are transferred from being ruled by the power of the old age to being ruled by the power of the Realm (Romans 6:1-23).

> One of the goals of the ministry of Christ is welcoming gentiles into the Realm of God.

To be sure, gentiles continue to struggle after baptism because gentile sin is powerful (Romans 7:1-25). Nevertheless, God has given the Spirit to gentiles to empower them in the struggle and to sustain them in the transition of the ages (Romans 8:1-39). As for the Jewish people themselves, they are called and destined for the Realm of God, and since God cannot break God's promises, "All Israel will be saved" (Romans 9:1–11:36). Since the gentile believers have been grafted onto Israel (and not the other way around), the gentiles should live in love with one another and with their Jewish sisters and brothers (Romans 12:1–15:13).

QUESTIONS FOR DISCUSSION

1. The chapter argues that Paul (like other writers of public letters) intended that these letters be read aloud. Ask someone in your group (or find a friend) to read a small part of a letter aloud so that you can *hear* it. What differences do you notice between the way you perceive the letter when you read it silently and when you hear it? One possible portion on which to try this might be Romans 12:14-21.

2. In this chapter did you come across surprises about Paul, or the situations in his congregations, or his advice to the congregations?

3. Paul addressed his letters to people in specific circumstances in the churches to which he wrote. Which of the circumstances in antiquity are similar to circumstances that your congregation faces?

4. Paul's method of thinking through a situation in antiquity can often help a congregation today. First, Paul described what was going on in a congregation. He then essentially asked: "Are the thoughts and behaviors in this congregation consistent with those of the Realm of God? Do the thoughts and behaviors of the congregation run against the grain of the Realm of God?" Paul then advised the congregation to make changes that would align their actual thoughts and behaviors with those of God's Realm. Perhaps you can think through an issue in your congregation using Paul's method: describe the circumstances, note where the congregation is similar to and different from the thoughts and values of the Realm, and what the congregation can do to become consistent with the Realm.

CHAPTER 8

The Four Gospels

In the contemporary film "Melinda and Melinda," the main action takes place at a table in a Manhattan restaurant where two guests — both writers — debate whether life is ultimately tragic (with a sad ending) or comic (with a happy ending). The writers tell the story of a single character (Melinda) in two different ways, one tragic and the other comic. The plot for the story is much the same in both versions, but the writers change details in order to give one version a tragic tone and the other version a comic twist.

Similarly, the Gospel writers — Matthew, Mark, Luke, and John — tell stories of Jesus, but do so in their own ways and for their own purposes. The differences among the four Gospels are not as great as the differences between the tragic and comic versions of Melinda's story, but each Gospel tells the story of Jesus with its own accents and shapes the story of Jesus to address the particular circumstances in that writer's congregation.

In this chapter, I describe the situation in the congregation that each writer addressed, the picture of Jesus in that Gospel, and what the Gospel writer hoped would happen in the congregation as a result of his writing. I also note some of the distinctive features of each Gospel.

Names, Dates, and Family Grouping among the Gospels

Most scholars today agree that the Gospel of Mark was written about 70 C.E. Matthew and Luke were written a little later (perhaps 80-90 C.E.). The Gospel of John was written about 90-95 C.E. I discuss the Gospels below in the order in which they were written to trace lines of development from Mark to Matthew and Luke.

The Gospels of Mark, Matthew, and Luke are part of these early Jewish discussions and seek to guide the churches in answering the question, "Where do we go without the temple?" Their answer: "We follow Jesus into the gentile mission as we await the Second Coming."

Although we use the names Matthew, Mark, Luke, and John to refer to the Gospel writers, we do not know for certain who wrote the actual documents. The church did not attach these names to the Gospels until decades after their writing, well into the second century C.E. While the names may derive from authentic memories, they might also have been added by later generations who sought to increase the authority the previously unnamed Gospels would have with the early church by associating the Gospels with the names of the historic figures of Jesus' earliest followers.

There are certain family resemblances among the Gospels. Mark wrote first. Matthew and Luke used Mark's outline of the story of Jesus while adding some passages from other ancient traditions and giving the material their own spins.[1] As I note below, the Gospel of John is quite different in tone and theology from the first three Gospels.

---

1. Scholars sometimes refer to Matthew, Mark, and Luke as the "synoptic Gospels." The word "synoptic" is from two Greek words that mean "to see together." When you look at the first three Gospels side by side in a book called a "synopsis," you can have a lot of fun comparing and contrasting how they tell the stories of Jesus. For a synopsis, see Appendix C (pp. 190-93).

The Destruction of the Temple: A Key Event

In response to a Jewish uprising, the Romans destroyed the temple in 70 C.E. This event — discussed further in Chapter 3 — was important to the formation of the Gospels, all of which were written after the destruction of the temple. That event raised major questions for the Gospel writers and for Judaism. Why did God allow the Romans to destroy the temple? With its major institution in ruins, what was the future of Judaism? Without the temple, what was essential to being Jewish? Who were reliable authorities for the new period?

After the destruction of the temple, the Jewish community at large passionately discussed these issues. The Gospels of Mark, Matthew, and Luke are part of these early Jewish discussions and seek to guide the churches in answering the question, "Where do we go without the temple?" Their answer: "We follow Jesus into the gentile mission as we await the Second Coming."

Mark

The situation of the congregation to whom Mark wrote. Mark wrote in the immediate wake of the destruction of the temple. Many scholars today think that Mark 13 is a window into the situation of Mark's community: they were faced with false messiahs (Mark 13:5-6, 21-22), ongoing violence (Mark 13:7-8), conflict with Jewish leaders (Mark 13:9-11), and discord in families (Mark 13:12-13). The Romans had set up a desolating sacrilege (an emblem of Caesar) in the ruins of the temple (Mark 13:14). Mark interpreted these situations as signs that the Second Coming was near. Indeed, according to Jesus, "There are some standing here who will not taste death until they see that the kingdom [Realm] of God has come with power" (Mark 9:1). The suffering of the community would increase as the Second Coming approached (Mark 13:17-20). Indeed, the author of Mark emphasizes that the suffering of the congregation to whom he writes is similar to the suffering of Jesus (Mark 8:31–9:1). Many in

Box 17. Traditional Authors of the Gospels

The first sources that name respected historic figures as authors of the Gospels are from the middle of the second century c.e. After the period of the New Testament, the church began to represent each Gospel writer with a different image. You sometimes see these images in church buildings, on book covers, or in other places.

- The Gospel of Matthew was said to be written by the figure named Matthew, listed as one of Jesus' original twelve apostles in the Gospels (Matthew 10:3; Mark 3:18; Luke 6:15; Acts 1:13). The church represents Matthew with an angel.
- The Gospel of Mark was said to be written by the Mark who was with Peter in Rome (1 Peter 5:13) or by John Mark (Acts 12:12, 25; 15:37-39) or possibly another early Mark mentioned in the New Testament (Colossians 4:10; 2 Timothy 4:11; Philemon 24). The church represents Mark with a lion.
- The Gospel of Luke and the book of Acts were said to be written by Luke, companion of Paul and beloved physician (Colossians 4:14; 2 Timothy 4:11; Philemon 24). Some authors have argued that Luke was a companion of Paul and is included in the "we" with which Luke narrates certain travels in the book of Acts (for example, Acts 16:9-18). The church represents Luke with an ox.
- The Gospel of John was said to be written by John the son of Zebedee from the list of Jesus' twelve disciples (Matthew 10:2; Mark 3:17; Luke 6:14; Acts 1:13). The Gospel of John refers to the "disciple whom Jesus loved" and might connect this disciple with the writing of the Gospel (John 19:26; 21:20-24). The church represents John with an eagle.

Any of these authorships is possible. However, none of the Gospels explicitly name their authors. As noted above, the earliest that the names of the Gospel writers are found in connection with the Gospels themselves is the middle of the second century — almost 100 years after the writing of the Gospels. Because people in antiquity valued things "of old," they may have attached these names to the Gospels in order to increase the authority of the Gospels in the church.

An ivory plaque showing representations of Matthew, Mark, Luke, and John surrounding Jesus, represented as the Lamb of God.

© The Metropolitan Museum of Art / Art Resource, NY

Mark's congregation were in danger of abandoning the community in order to escape their suffering.

The picture of Jesus in the Gospel of Mark. Mark pictures Jesus as an end-time preacher in the tradition of John the Baptist. The major difference between John and Jesus (according to Mark) is that God chose Jesus not only to announce the end of the present world and the coming of the Realm of God but also to be God's active agent through whom God actually begins to bring about his Realm in the here and now.

What Mark hoped would happen when the congregation heard this Gospel. Mark urged the community to be faithful until the Second Coming so that they would be a part of the new world (Mark 13:24-27). He wants the community to do what Jesus did: faithfully endure their season of suffering so that they will be ready to welcome the Realm of God. While awaiting the end, the community is to witness to the presence and coming of the Realm, including engaging in the gentile mission (Mark 13:10). Mark presents Jesus as reinterpreting some long-standing Jewish traditions in view of the imminence of the coming of the Realm of God.

Mark wants the community to do what Jesus did: faithfully endure their season of suffering so that they will be ready to welcome the Realm of God.

Distinctive features. Mark does not include the story of the birth of Jesus but begins the story of Jesus with the preaching of John the Baptist. The Gospel of Mark is charged with a sense of urgency. He repeatedly uses the word "immediately" to move his readers with a sense of urgency to remain faithful to Jesus through their crises.

Matthew

The situation of the congregation to whom Matthew wrote. Matthew likely wrote to a congregation located in the area of either Lebanon or Syria today. Matthew's community faced adversities similar to that of Mark's congregation but with three differences. First, many in Matthew's congregation were losing confidence that Jesus would return. The second major difference from Mark's situation comes as a surprise to many readers today. Matthew himself was likely a Pharisee who believed that Jesus was God's agent bringing about the Realm. I interpret Matthew's congregation as a Pharisaic synagogue who shared this belief.[2] In my view, his congregation was in conflict with nearby Pharisaic synagogues regarding how to interpret Jewish and Pharisaic traditions faithfully. Synagogues in Matthew's neighborhood charged that his group was no longer truly Jewish. Third, Matthew's congregation had some difficult internal conflicts.

The picture of Jesus in the Gospel of Matthew. Not surprisingly, in view of the situation just described, Matthew presents Jesus as a rabbi (a Jewish teacher) who instructs the community to be prepared to live through a delay in the Second Coming and to relate traditional Jewish teaching to the end of the world and the coming of the Realm of God. We might call Jesus an end-time rabbi. Jesus' teachings in Matthew are designed to help the community respond appropriately to the presence of the Realm of God.

What Matthew hoped would happen when the congregation heard this Gospel. Matthew wants his congregation not only to continue to look forward to the Second Coming but actively to witness to the Realm of God as they do so. Jesus admonishes the disciples not only to hear his words but also to act on them (Matthew 7:24-27). For example, Jesus tells a series of parables to motivate the community to witness as they await Jesus' return. They are to be faithful servants, to keep their lamps lit, to multiply their talents, and to care for the

Jesus admonishes the disciples not only to hear his words but also to act on them.

---

2. Other interpreters view Matthew's congregation as made up of Jewish and gentile believers but not being Pharisaic. Matthew's congregation was then in tension with the Pharisees (and perhaps other Jewish groups). In a memorable phrase, interpreters sometimes say that Matthew's community was in debate with "the synagogue across the street." In any event, most scholars today think that Matthew sought to assure his community that they were authentically Jewish in the face of other Jewish groups who claimed that Matthew's group was abandoning Judaism.

hungry, thirsty, strangers, naked, sick, and imprisoned (Matthew 24:45–25:46).

Matthew urges the congregation to recognize that they are fully and faithfully Jewish. From his point of view, Jesus' message is from the heart of Judaism (Matthew 5:17-20). Jesus objects not to Judaism as such but to the fact that some of the Pharisees nearby do not follow the best of their own tradition (Matthew 23:1-3). In this context, Jesus' interpretation of Jewish tradition is trustworthy because God has authorized Jesus as God's end-time rabbi.

Matthew wants the internal life of his congregation to embody the Realm of God. This includes going after members who are in danger of drifting away and exercising pastoral discipline over those who disrupt the community (Matthew 18:1-35).

In antiquity, the last words of a character were key to understanding that character, and that is especially so in Matthew. Jesus' final words to the church inaugurated the mission to make disciples of the gentiles (nations) by teaching and baptizing until Jesus returns at the end of the age. In the meantime, the risen Jesus would always be with them (Matthew 28:16-20).

Distinctive features. Matthew begins with a genealogy that employs traditional end-of-time Jewish symbolism to show that Jesus was born in the climactic generation when the apocalypse will occur. This is suggested by the structure of the genealogy, which organizes the generations into groups of fourteen members with Jesus at the pinnacle. Matthew tells the birth of Jesus and the story of the coming of the three astrologers from the East (the wise men), but leaves out the story of the shepherds. His Gospel contains the famous Sermon on the Mount (Matthew 5–7). Matthew is the only Gospel to use the word "church" to identify Jesus' followers (Matthew 16:18; 18:15-17).

Luke-Acts

The same author not only wrote both the Gospel of Luke and the book of Acts, but he saw them telling *one continuous story.* We should not focus on the Gospel of Luke alone, but we should read Luke-Acts as one ongoing narrative. To understand Luke's full meaning, we should follow how he unpacks the story and its themes from the Gospel of Luke into the book of Acts.

Luke's congregation was located in an urban area outside of Palestine. Luke had a thorough knowledge of Judaism, especially its sacred scriptures.

The situation of the congregation to whom Luke wrote. Luke's congregation was discouraged about the delay of the Second Coming. They struggled with some Jewish authorities over the issue of whether they adhered sufficiently to Jewish tradition. Indeed, members of Luke's congregation wrestled among themselves with the question of how many Jewish attitudes and behaviors gentiles needed to take on when they joined the church (Acts 15:1-29). The wealthy in the congregation did not share their resources with the poor (see, for example, Luke 16:19-31; Acts 2:42-47). Some people evidently questioned whether women should be in positions of leadership (see Luke 8:1-3; Acts 2:17-18).

The picture of Jesus in the Gospel of Luke and the book of Acts. Luke sees Jesus as a prophet in the tradition of Old Testament prophets such as Elijah and Elisha. He understands the suffering of Jesus to be in line with the suffering of the prophets in the Old Testament. For Luke the ascension was the climax of the earthly ministry of Jesus, that moment when Jesus rises from earth into heaven. Since Jesus, according to the book of Acts, is now at the right hand of God, he rules over all other rulers (including Caesar) (Acts 1:1-11). That is why Luke calls Jesus "Savior": Jesus saves people from the old age for the age of the Realm of God.

What Luke hoped would happen when the congregation heard the Gospel of Luke and the book of Acts. Luke wanted his congregation to remain full of vigor during the prolonged delay of Jesus' return. He wanted them to know that God sent the same Spirit who strengthened Jesus during his ministry to the church on the Day of Pentecost. The Spirit would empower the church to be a witness to the world during the extended wait for the Second Coming. Luke describes an apostolic conference in which Paul and the other apostles concluded that gentiles who joined the church had to "abstain from what has been sacrificed to idols and from blood and from what is strangled and from fornication" (Acts 15:29). These basic compromises would facilitate Jews and gentiles getting along in the congregation. Luke also wanted the members of the community to share their material resources with one another so that none were in need. He believed that the gentile mission was the future of his community (Luke 24:44-49; Acts 9:1-19; 10:1–11:18; 28:23-28). Indeed, for Luke, the gentile mission was the goal of the story of Israel. In the present, awaiting the full unveiling of the Realm of God, Luke suggests that the community recognize that while God would ultimately condemn the Roman Empire, God could use representatives of the empire for divine purposes, such as when Roman authorities protected Paul from mob violence. The basic stance of the church would be to stay out of the way of the empire.

God sent the Spirit to the church on the Day of Pentecost. The Spirit would empower the church to be a witness to the world during the extended wait for the Second Coming.

Distinctive features. Luke alone mentions the coming of the shepherds to the manger in the story of the birth of Jesus. Luke-Acts repeatedly emphasizes the importance of prayer in the life of Jesus and of the early church. Luke alone continues the story of Jesus by telling it and pairing it with the story of the earliest followers, the apostles, and the beginning of the mission to the gentiles.

John

Differences between the Gospel of John and the Gospels of Matthew, Mark, and Luke. Whereas Paul, Mark, Matthew, and Luke look to the end of time as the fulfillment of God's plan, the Gospel of John was written with a different understanding. John saw the world divided into two spheres that we can describe figuratively as a two-story house: God in heaven (upstairs) and human beings in the world (downstairs). For John, heaven is the sphere of life, light, truth, and freedom whereas the world simply means: "not heaven." The world is not just the place where we happen to live; it is the sphere of death, darkness, falsehood, and slavery. John's narrative is not concerned with the end of the present world but rather with what happens within this world serving as a prelude to joining Jesus in heaven with God.

> **John's narrative is not concerned with the end of the present world but rather with what happens within this world serving as a prelude to joining Jesus in heaven with God.**

The situation of the congregation to whom John wrote. The situation of John's congregation was similar that of Matthew's congregation. John's community was a synagogue that believed in Jesus as the one who most completely revealed God. They were in tension with other Jewish groups. Indeed, a nearby synagogue had cast out or excommunicated John's congregation (John 9:22, 34). Many in the congregation questioned whether they were still faithfully Jewish. It seems as well that the members of the congregation were divided among themselves. This situation would account for the many calls to love one another found in the Gospel of John (for example, John 13:34-35; 14:15-24).

The picture of Jesus in the Gospel of John. The picture of Jesus in the Gospel of John is tied to John's understanding of the world described above (the two-storied house). Before the coming of Jesus, John thought that people were trapped in the world of death and darkness and had only limited knowledge of God. But God sent Jesus from heaven into the world to reveal that God loves the world. The essential work of Jesus in the Gospel of John is to reveal that God loves the world. Jesus performs this revealing work through his words, through signs or miracles, and through encounters with other people who either receive or reject the work of God he comes to do (for example, John 3:11-21, 31-36).

What John hoped would happen when the congregation heard this Gospel. John describes Jesus assuring his followers that they are truly Jewish and that Jesus' interpretation of Judaism is authoritative because it comes from God. In fact, according to John, the Jewish people who did not follow Jesus did not understand their own faith and were cut off from God (John 3:16-21). Indeed, Jewish people who do not acknowledge God's revelation in Jesus are children of the devil rather than children of Sarah and Abraham (the founding father and mother of the Jewish people; John 8:39-47).

People who believe in Jesus experience heaven while they continue to live in the world. They live in the sphere of heaven even though a dying world is all around them. At a future time, perhaps at death, they will follow Jesus into the fullness of heaven (John 14:1-7). John repeatedly stresses that until then the disciples are to love one another since that is the way of heaven (John 13:31-35; 15:12-16).

Whereas Paul, Mark, Matthew, and Luke all stress that the gentile mission is integral to the future of their congregations, the Gospel of John does not directly advocate a gentile mission. Indeed, scholars sometimes speak of this Gospel as "sectarian" in the sense that it describes the congregation as a small and closely knit community whose members care for one another and have little mission in the outside world.

Distinctive features. John does not tell the story of the birth of Jesus but goes much farther back. For John, Jesus existed as the "Word" in heaven with God aeons before Jesus' birth as a human being. When John speaks of "the Jews," he is not talking about the Jewish people in general but of those Jewish leaders who opposed John's congregation. Whereas Matthew, Mark, and Luke depict Jesus as speaking in short, pithy sayings and telling parables, John pictures Jesus speaking in long, flowing discourses. Where the first three Gospels speak of miracles, John uses the word "signs" for the same phenomenon. The chronology of Jesus' ministry in John is different than it is in Matthew, Mark, and Luke.

Box 18. Some Comparisons in the Chronology of Matthew, Mark, and Luke with John

While Matthew, Mark, and Luke present the sequence of events in Jesus' life with many similarities, the Gospel of John is rather different. I have space in the following chart to mention only some highlights. Of course, there are also some differences among Matthew, Mark, and Luke.

	Matthew, Mark, & Luke	John
Length of Jesus' ministry	About one year	About three years
Location of Jesus' ministry	In the first part of the Gospels, Jesus is mostly in Galilee, but also goes to Jerusalem.	Jesus is located largely in Judea and near Jerusalem, from which he occasionally goes to Galilee.
First miracle	Exorcism of the demoniac in the synagogue at Capernaum (Mark 1:23-28; Luke 4:33-37)	Turning the water to wine at the wedding in Cana (John 2:1-11)
Visits to Jerusalem	Jesus makes only one visit to Jerusalem.	Several extended visits to Jerusalem
Cleansing of the temple	Takes place at the beginning of the last week of Jesus (Matthew 21:12-13; Mark 11:15-17; Luke 19:45-46)	Takes place very near the beginning of Jesus' ministry (John 2:13-24)
Jewish feasts	The only Jewish feast mentioned is Passover.	Jesus attends several feasts (5:1; 7:2-52; 10:22-39).
Passover	Jesus attends only one Passover observance (when he is killed).	Jesus attends three Passover observances (John 2:13; 13:1).
The last supper	Takes place in the context of the Passover meal in Jerusalem	Takes place before the day of preparation; does not mention bread and cup (John 13:1-30)
The death of Jesus	Takes place on Passover	Takes place on the day of preparation (the day before Passover)

QUESTIONS FOR DISCUSSION

1. Based on the brief summaries in this chapter, to which Gospel(s) are you most attracted — Mark, Matthew, Luke-Acts, or John? What about that Gospel attracts you?

2. Mark believed that the Realm of God would come before his life ended. What would you say about the fact that the Realm of God has not occurred at the time or in the way Mark envisioned?

3. The Gospels of Matthew and Luke both assume a delay between the resurrection and the Second Coming, and they counsel readers to witness for the Realm of God while waiting for it. Do you think that we are still in such a delay? If so, what do you think we should do during the wait? If you do not believe we are in a delay, what do you think about the meaning of the Second Coming for us today? What should we do if we do not believe that the Second Coming will occur?

4. The Gospel of John claims that human beings can experience aspects of heaven while still in the world. Can you describe a time when you believe that you experienced a bit of John's heaven in your life?

CHAPTER 9

The Letters of Paul's Disciples (?)

Now we will explore six letters in the New Testament that, at first blush, seem to be written by Paul: Colossians, Ephesians, 2 Thessalonians, 1 and 2 Timothy, and Titus. Each of these letters' opening words is similar to the ones found in Colossians. "Paul, an apostle of Christ Jesus by the will of God . . . To the saints and faithful brothers and sisters in Christ in Colossae" (Colossians 1:1-2).

Of course you would think that such a beginning means that the letters are from Paul. However, as the question mark at the end of this chapter's title indicates, scholars disagree whether Paul was the author. One group of scholars thinks that some or all of these letters bear the name of Paul but were actually written by some of Paul's followers. As indicated earlier in the book, I share this viewpoint. Another group of scholars argues that since these letters begin and end with Paul's name (and contain a few other references to Paul's life), the letters must be from Paul himself.

In today's culture, forgery is the name we usually give to one person writing in another person's name. Forgery is not only dishonest but can be a crime. Why should we take seriously, let alone accept, ancient documents whose authorship is a lie? In the ancient world, however, the phenomenon of disciples writing in the name of a master was not uncommon nor improper. Further, the church has always found the counsel of these letters trustworthy even if they do not come directly from Paul.

In the first century, it would have been looked upon as perfectly acceptable for a disciple to write in the name of a master or teacher. This mitigates our choices. The letters do not have to be either from Paul or be forgeries. This historical fact is one of the main reasons why many scholars think that these letters come from a hand other than Paul's. Each letter can be read, therefore, with an eye toward the situation that prompted its writing without being limited to interpretations that would be necessary had Paul himself written them. We can now ask what the letter writer sought to accomplish with that letter and study the distinctive features of the letter.

Scholars sometimes refer to these letters as "Deutero-Pauline." The designation "deutero" means "second," and refers to these letters as coming from the second generation after Paul's ministry.

Disciples Writing in the Name of a Teacher

In antiquity, it was fairly common for a student or follower to write in the name of a teacher or leader, especially after the master or teacher was dead. The disciples encountered new situations that their teacher had not directly addressed. Since the student was trained in the thinking of the teacher, the student could apply the teacher's perspectives to new situations. Such student writers created letters and other documents that reflected the spirit of the teacher while bringing new expressions and even some new ideas to bear on the fresh circumstances.

In antiquity, it was fairly common for a student or follower to write in the name of a teacher or leader, especially after the master or teacher was dead.

From time to time such a writer could be an admirer of sorts even if they had not directly studied with the figure whose name they were borrowing. Such writings could be accepted by the followers of a great teacher except, of course, when the "ghost" writer grossly violated the original teachings or the values of the community.

Box 19. Some Documents Written in the Names of Others

Here are some documents from antiquity that were written by disciples in the name of their teachers or that were written by a later generation in the name of an earlier figure.

Prayer of Nabonidas
Psalms of Solomon
1 Enoch
2 Baruch
Odes of Solomon
Ascension of Isaiah
3 Corinthians
Apocalypse of Peter

These documents are only a few of the many that were accepted as authoritative by some groups in the ancient world.

This practice is not entirely foreign to our own time. Here is an everyday example. When I was a graduate student in the 1970s, one of my friends worked as an assistant to a professor who had a lot of correspondence. This correspondence often related to speaking engagements, study groups, or to his publications. In those "good old days" correspondence consisted of writing letters on pieces of paper and mailing them through the U.S. Post Office. My friend wrote virtually all of the professor's letters. Sometimes the professor would suggest the general content of a letter, but much of the time my friend composed the letter. Since the graduate assistant had taken several courses with the professor and read all the professor's books, the assistant not only had a good idea about the way the professor would approach many topics but could use vocabulary and sentence structure similar to that of the professor. From time to time, my friend signed the professor's name to letters.

Arguments for and against Paul's Authorship

The following are the leading reasons why many scholars think that Paul did not write the letters we are discussing here. The arguments stem from comparisons of the seven letters we know certainly came from Paul with these six whose authorship is disputed.

- Some of the word choices are very different from each other in the two groups of letters.
- There are differences in sentence structure and style between the two groups of letters.
- Some of the ideas in the first group of letters are different from those in the other group.
- The organizational structure of the churches being addressed seems to be more developed in the six disputed letters than in the seven undisputed ones.

At the same time, scholars acknowledge that these arguments are not watertight. I imagine that you know people who, over time and in different circumstances, change their language and even their views. It is possible that Paul expressed himself in different ways at different moments in his life, and that his views changed as he gave further thought to particular issues and situations. As I emphasized at the beginning of this chapter, whether or not the letters come from Paul, the church has always believed that they provide wise counsel.

Developments in the Pauline Tradition

Some scholars perceive changes in perspective in these later letters from that found in the letters understood to be certainly from Paul. Further, these later documents differ from each other on some key points.

- Paul himself thought the Second Coming would occur soon. These later six letters urge readers to continue to be ready for the Second Coming, but also to be prepared for a long delay.

- These six letters reflect Paul's thinking that the Realm of God will come only after Jesus returns, but they also pay more attention to salvation as a present experience.
- The later writers reflect more of a Greek way of thinking and Greek cultural expectations for life than do the original letters from Paul.
- Although Paul reflects traditional attitudes regarding the superiority of men to women, he sees that relationship moving toward the equality that God intended in Eden (Galatians 3:28), whereas the later letters begin to move in the direction of reflecting their culture's understanding of male superiority, though some scholars are coming to think that the later letters contain more liberating elements than may at first appear to the casual reader.
- The congregations to whom Paul wrote were loosely organized, whereas these later congregations (especially 1 and 2 Timothy and Titus) are much more highly structured.

Colossians

The problem in the church at Colossae that prompted this letter was that an outside "philosophy" had begun to influence the community (Colossians 2:8). According to this philosophy, part of the self would leave the body to seek visions of the heavenly world. Indeed, for people to have such visions (and thereby to commune with God), they needed to subdue the body by fasting, eating only certain foods, and observing special (unnamed) holidays, and worship angels (Colossians 1:16-23). The philosophy denied that the work of God through Christ had been sufficient for them. It also denied the value of their physical existence both in the present and in the future life.

In response, Paul or Paul's student charged that such philosophy came from "elemental spirits of the universe," that is, powers similar to demons. These powers wanted to wrestle control of human beings away from God (Colossians 2:8, 20-23). To accept this invading philosophy was to return to bondage to these elemental spirits. The author quoted an early Christian hymn in Colossians 1:15-20 to remind the Colossians that God through Christ had already freed them from elemental spirits and that they were experiencing salvation in their bodies — which were good — in the present.

The Colossians had already "been raised with [Christ]" and did not need additional ecstatic visions. Instead, they needed to put into practice the values and practices of the Realm that God had already given to them. Many of the later sections of the letter give practical advice on how to behave consistently with the Realm of God (Colossians 3:1–4:5). The behaviors the author affirms support the fact that God's redemption is a re-creation of the body and the physical world, not an escape from the physical. Colossians affirms that God through Christ is body- and world-affirming while the philosophy of the "elemental spirits" was denying both body and world.

> **Colossians affirms that God through Christ is body- and world-affirming while the philosophy of the "elemental spirits" was denying both body and world.**

Ephesians

The letter to the Ephesians presents us with a puzzle. In most English translations, Ephesians 1:1 reads, "Paul, an apostle of Christ Jesus . . . To the saints who are in Ephesus and are faithful in Christ Jesus." You would think that this letter was obviously written to the congregation at Ephesus. However, some of the oldest manuscripts — the surviving parchment copies on which we base our current editions of the New Testament — omit the words "in Ephesus." The lack of the words "in Ephesus" has given rise to the idea that this letter was not originally written to one specific congregation but was intended as a traveling letter to be read aloud in a number of congregations.

We cannot identify any one specific event or issue that prompted this letter as precisely as we can in the case of Colossians or 2 Thessalonians (below). Ephesians is addressed primarily to gentiles who have left gentile religions behind and have become followers of the God of Israel through the work of Jesus Christ. It may be that some of the congregations the author had in mind struggled with questions about the relationships between Jewish and gentile peoples and about the connections of the gentile followers of Jesus with their former gentile religions and behaviors.

In the thanksgiving paragraph, the author employs a Jewish form of prayer, called a blessing, reminding the gentiles that they now belong to the God of Israel (Ephesians 1:3-23). After describing their desperate situation before conversion (Ephesians 2:1-10), the author reminds the gentiles that God has brought them into relationship with Israel and God. Note that the Jewish people did not make a change. Rather, the gentiles who had been "aliens from the commonwealth of Israel, and strangers to the covenants of promise" are now grafted in with the Jewish people. Now the gentiles are no longer strangers and aliens, but "citizens with the saints and also members of the household of God" (Ephesians 2:11-22).

That Jewish and gentile believers are one reflects the oneness of God.

In that sense, the gentiles have become more Jewish. Such movement is in accordance with God's plan to bring the gentiles into the fullness of God's realm (Ephesians 3:1-21). That Jewish and gentile believers are one reflects the oneness of God and is a call to gentiles outside the church (Ephesians 4:1-16). Consequently, the gentiles in the church need to refrain from behavior that will destroy community, the very behavior of the unconverted gentile world (Ephesians 4:1–6:9). Gentile believers need to recognize that their life in Christ is a struggle against the principalities and powers, the very forces imbedded in human reality that would keep the gentile world in ignorance and turmoil (Ephesians 6:10-17). According to the author of Ephesians, Christ has defeated these powers and therefore urges the congregations reading this letter to more fully align themselves with Christ and not with the fading powers of the gentile world.

2 Thessalonians

Part of the situation that prompted this letter to be written is that some of the believers in Thessalonica were so enthusiastic about Jesus' return and their hope that it was going to occur very soon that they had given up their employment. They believed that the Second Coming was going to take place at any moment. Hence they did not think they needed to work any longer (2 Thessalonians 3:6-15). Many in the community were idle. Another part of the situation that gave rise to this letter is that the community was suffering. It is likely that this congregation, made up largely of converted gentiles, was being harassed by unconverted gentiles who found these new converts' change of life unsettling (2 Thessalonians 1:4).

On the one hand, the author of 2 Thessalonians agreed with the congregation that Jesus would return. On the other, this writer urged the congregation to recognize that the Second Coming of Jesus was delayed (2 Thessalonians 2:1-3). Like other Jewish and Christian writers in antiquity who concerned themselves with the end of time, the author of 2 Thessalonians thought that God had planned a set sequence of events that would take place before the big finish or apocalypse (2 Thessalonians 2:1-12). This author used this extended time line to urge the congregation to take responsibility for living and witnessing faithfully in the current period (2 Thessalonians 2:13–3:5; 3:14), as the end was not so very soon. In particular, they were to work hard to support themselves and not become idle (2 Thessalonians 3:6-13). By living appropriately to their time in history, the Thessalonians would be ready to face the final judgment when Christ did return (2 Thessalonians 1:5-12).

By living appropriately to their time in history, the Thessalonians would be ready to face the final judgment when Christ did return.

1 and 2 Timothy and Titus

These three books were written in the same general time frame and to similar circumstances. They are sometimes called "the pastoral epistles" or "the pastoral letters" because the author writes to Timothy and Titus as "pastors" of local congregations.

The issues that prompted these letters to be written seem to have a family resemblance to problems we found addressed in the letter to the Colossians. False teachers had visited the communities. These teachers passed along "myths and endless genealogies." The upshot of their influence was that people in these communities had stopped marrying and needlessly abstained from some foods (1 Timothy 1:3-7; 4:1-5; Titus 1:10-16). Some visitors to these congregations taught that the resurrection had already occurred. The writer calls this "idle talk." These new teachers were, to the mind of the writer of these pastoral letters, remarkably self-centered (2 Timothy 2:16-18, 23-26; 3:2-5).

According to the author, the congregations should avoid the false teachers and should adhere to "sound teaching" (1 Timothy 1:10; 3:14-16; 4:16; 6:2-10; 2 Timothy 1:13-14; 4:3; Titus 1:9, 13; 2:1, 2, 8). This author assumed that the churches had developed a recognized body of authoritative doctrine ("sound teaching"). Further, the writer assumed that the churches had a well-developed structure of leadership, including elders (or bishops) and deacons, in each congregation (1 Timothy 3:1-13; 5:17-22; Titus 1:5-9).

The primary work of the elder or bishop was to clarify the sound teaching already received and to help the congregation embrace that teaching. The members of the congregation should ignore the false teachers and turn instead to the elders for trustworthy guidance (1 Timothy 5:1–6:19; 2 Timothy 2:1-26; 3:10-17; Titus 2:1–3:11).

QUESTIONS FOR DISCUSSION

1. How do you respond to the possibility that the letters discussed in this chapter may not have been written by Paul but by one of Paul's students?

2. The philosophy at Colossae taught that the body got in the way of spiritual life. People who followed that philosophy sought to subdue the body in order to achieve communion with God. The writer of Colossians, on the other hand, taught that God will redeem us in our bodies, that God communes with us through bodies, and that we can use our bodies to create the kind of world here that is already in place in heaven. What are some things you can do to align your own life and congregation more closely with the world above?

3. Read Ephesians 4:25–5:2. Can you identify a situation in your own life or in your experience that connects to this passage? For example, community-undermining gossip is a problem in some congregations. This passage admonishes such churches, "Let no evil talk come out of your mouths, but only what is useful for building up" (Ephesians 4:29). At what points do you hear this passage speaking to your congregation?

4. Paul believed that through the event of Jesus Christ God was ending the hierarchy of men over women that had prevailed since the fall (Genesis 3:16). "In Christ," Paul says, "there is no longer male and female" (Galatians 3:28). Several non-Pauline letters discussed in this chapter reflect more of their culture's understanding that wives are to be subject to their husbands (Colossians 3:18; Ephesians 5:22-24; 1 Timothy 2:11-15; Titus 2:3-5) while retaining important elements of Paul's insight. For example, Ephesians 5:21 urges spouses to "be subject to one another" and 5:25-33 urges husbands to love their wives even as Christ loves the church. What can the church today do to help extend these impulses toward mutuality into relationships between women and men?

CHAPTER 10

Other New Testament Writings

To this point in the book, we have discussed individual New Testament writings, considering their place within a larger stream of documents according to authorship or subject matter. We have examined the letters written by Paul and in Paul's name, and the Gospels, which all tell the story of Jesus. Now we come to nine documents whose primary common characteristic is that they were written in the same general time frame (from 80 C.E. to 110 C.E.). We encounter at least six authors here. These writings contain four types of literature: Hebrews is most likely a sermon; James, 1 Peter, Jude, and 1, 2, and 3 John are letters; 2 Peter has all the markings of a last will and testament; the book of Revelation is a vision of the end time also known as an Apocalypse. The documents in this chapter derive from different views of the world. Hebrews and 1, 2, and 3 John share with the Gospel of John a two-story understanding of the world (see pp. 114-15). The other books are largely shaped by a consciousness deeply aware of the end of time and a belief that it is nearing.

As in the previous chapters, I report both the circumstances in the congregation that provoked the author to put quill to parchment as well as the purpose the document serves for the community it addresses. What did the writers want to happen when the congregations read each of these books?

Hebrews

At one time, many Christians thought that Hebrews (or "To the Hebrews") was a letter written by Paul. However, the book is not written in the form of a letter, and the text never names Paul as the author. Today, many scholars agree that Hebrews is a sermon.

Before turning to the sermon itself, I need to say a word about the view of the world of the congregation to whom Hebrews was addressed. The congregation appears to share a two-story view of the universe similar to that of the Gospel of John (see pp. 114-15) and several other early Jewish groups. The goal of those practicing this form of Judaism was for the soul to leave the earth (the lower story) and make its way to heaven (the upper story) where it would live in the immediate presence of God.

Hebrews' claim is that Jesus is the one who leads people from earth to heaven. However, some people within the congregation questioned whether Jesus could accomplish that task. An unnamed Christian preacher prepared Hebrews as a sermon to reassure the congregation that Jesus was trustworthy to lead them to heaven.

> **Hebrews' claim is that Jesus is the one who leads people from earth to heaven.**

The writer sometimes refers to the state of being in heaven with God as being "perfect" or reaching "perfection" (for example, Hebrews 2:10; 5:9; 7:11, 19, 28; 9:11; 10:1; 11:40; 12:23).

For Hebrews, Jesus is "the pioneer and perfecter of our faith" (Hebrews 12:2). He is the pioneer because he leads the way from earth to heaven. He is the perfecter because he is the one who makes it possible for human beings to become perfect, that is, to be with God in heaven. Jesus was made perfect through suffering (Hebrews 2:10). For Hebrews, suffering works like a refiner's fire in metallurgy that purges impurities from the metal. These impurities would keep the self earthbound and prevent the journey to heaven.

The writer assures readers that Jesus can lead them to glory (another word for heaven or perfection) by showing the superiority of Jesus to Judaism for that task. Thus, Hebrews is mostly a series of comparisons between Jesus and the angels (Hebrews 1:5-14), Moses (3:1-6), Joshua (4:1-11), the Jewish priests (4:14–5:10; 7:1-28), and the old covenant with its sacrifices and worship (8:1–10:18). Since Jesus is superior to Judaism, the congregation should endure their suffering in order to receive salvation (Hebrews 10:19–12:1; 12:4-13). In so doing, they would follow the example of Jesus (Hebrews 12:2-3, 12-14).

1, 2, and 3 John

Although these letters bear the name John in the English versions of the Bible, the name John does not appear in them, and we do not know the name of their author for certain. Their language and beliefs are so similar to those of the Gospel of John that scholars conclude that the letters and the Gospel come from the same circle.

Like 1 and 2 Timothy and Titus (discussed in the previous chapter), the three letters of John were written about the same time and to similar situations. They do differ slightly. While 1 John lacks some of the formal characteristics of a letter, most scholars think that it is a public letter addressed to a congregation. 2 John is a personal letter addressed to the same congregation. The congregation is addressed as "the elect lady" (2 John 1). 3 John is a personal letter to an individual in the congregation named Gaius.

What prompted the writing of these letters? The situation to which the Gospel of John was addressed provides a clue. The congregation was made up of Jewish people who had come to believe that Jesus revealed God's love for the world and opened a way for people who believe in him to go from the world into the presence of God. But some people in the synagogue not only claimed that Jesus' followers could not hold this belief, but also excommunicated John's group from the synagogue.

The author wrote the letters of John because some members had left the congregation under unhappy circumstances (1 John 2:19). What was their problem? Evidently they had lost confidence that Jesus was the Christ and had returned to the synagogue (1 John

2:22-23; 4:2-3; 2 John 7). Their departure had been contentious and had disrupted the life of the congregation.

The author assures the congregation that Jesus did, in fact, come from God and that the revelation from God through Jesus is trustworthy and opens the way from the world to the presence of God (1 John 1:5; 2:2; 2:28–3:3; 4:1-6; 5:1-12). Moreover, in its ruptured and painful condition, the congregation needed to obey the commandments that Jesus gave, the most important of which was to love one another (1 John 2:3-6; 3:11-24; 4:7-21; 2 John 4-10). However, like the Gospel of John, the letters are sectarian. The writer's admonition to love is aimed at sisters and brothers in the community (1 John 2:7-11). Those who do not love and do not confess Jesus are guilty of sin (1 John 3:4-10).

James

The book of James has had a rocky history in the church. Many Christians have thought that the author was a brother of Jesus (Galatians 1:19; Acts 15:13; 21:18). While that is possible, most scholars think that this letter was written by someone using James's name, as with the letters written in the name of Paul. Beyond that, Martin Luther, a church leader in the 1500s, had a dim view of James because it teaches "works-righteousness," that is, a person needs to perform good acts or works to be saved, to be with God. Luther preferred Paul, whom Luther interpreted as teaching that we are saved only by grace — a gift from God that is not earned — through faith — simply in the act of believing. Today, however, a good many scholars think that Luther misunderstood both James and Paul. Most scholars today argue that what Paul meant by faith was that people needed to believe that God is bringing about his Realm through Christ and to live accordingly. This in fact is fairly close to what the author of James meant by "faith and works."

The congregation to which James was written was made up of people who were Jewish in background and who believed that God was bringing about the Realm through Christ. Many in the congregation thought that having such faith was all they needed in antici-pation of Jesus' return. Confident of their place in the coming Realm of God, they neglected to live in ways that were consistent with the Realm. James implies that the community showed favorit-ism to the wealthy while disparaging the poor (James 2:1-7), even while the rich did not exercise care for the poor (James 5:1-6). James contends further that many people were talking inappropriately about one another, even passing judgment on one another (James 3:1-12; 4:11-12). His community acted as if they were the masters of their own destinies and did not have a proper respect for God's rule in their lives (James 4:13-17). They were in danger of being unfaith-ful to God in the midst of their suffering (James 5:7-11).

The writer admonishes the community to remember that they will be judged at the Second Coming on the basis of both faith and works (James 2:14-26). The writer of James does not, however, con-firm Luther's charge that James taught that a person is made right with God by doing good deeds (works-righteousness). In the Jewish tradition, faith and works are not two separate activities but are in continuity with each other. The way a person believes should determine how that person acts. God will save the members of the congregation only if they combine confidence in the Second Coming with lives that embody the qualities of the Realm of God. Thus, James directs the congregation not to favor the wealthy (James 2:1-7), to talk in ways that build up the community (James 3:1-12; 4:11-12), to respect God's control of their life possibilities (James 4:13-16), and to be patient in their suffering (James 5:7-11).

1 Peter

Although both 1 and 2 Peter were written in the name of Peter — the central figure among Jesus' twelve apostles — most scholars today think that the letters were written long after the original Peter passed from the scene. Seeing the titles 1 and 2 Peter, you might think that they are some kind of one-two punch to a given congregation. However, the letters are so different that scholars think they address different situations. That is why each letter gets its own section here.

The letter of 1 Peter envisions the congregation as a community of "exiles" or "aliens" (1 Peter 1:1; 2:11). In the past many interpreted this to mean that the church was in exile from heaven. In recent years, scholars have recognized that the church being addressed in 1 Peter was a community that lived in exile within its own culture. Further, some scholars even think that Peter's community was made up almost entirely of resident aliens. 1 Peter in this case is addressed to people who came from one community but resided in another without having been fully embraced by their new community. As an analogy, you might think of laborers from Mexico working and living in the United States. Although such Mexicans are in the United States, large portions of American culture often harass them.

The community was therefore suffering, thus intensifying the general experience of exile (1 Peter 2:18-25; 3:13-22; 4:12-19). Like some of the other faith communities in the New Testament at which we have looked, they may have suffered as a result of conversion — gentiles abandoning their traditional gods and religions to follow the God of Israel as preached by the early church. As these gentiles withdrew from certain aspects of their society, their neighbors might not have appreciated the change and might have harassed them. Not surprisingly, the congregation was confused about its identity, and some members were in danger of drifting away from their Christian faith to escape this suffering.

> They are truly exiles, that is, cut off from their final homeland — the Realm of God.

The writer encourages members of the community to endure in the face of suffering. They are truly exiles, that is, cut off from their final homeland — the Realm of God that will be fully brought about at the Second Coming of Jesus. If they persist faithfully until then, God will welcome them into the Realm (1 Peter 1:3-25). Indeed, in the midst of exile, God has called them to active witness to their parent culture (1 Peter 2:1-12).

The author of 1 Peter also urges his readers to convince the unconverted gentiles that the latter had nothing to fear from the church as a means of bringing an end to the harassment the church had received (1 Peter 2:11-12). The congregation seemed willing to go to great lengths to prove to their neighbors that they were acceptable citizens, including fully cooperating with the Roman Empire (1 Peter 2:13-17) and following the conventional roles assigned to slaves, wives, and husbands (1 Peter 2:18–3:7) rather than the codes of conduct better suited to the new Christian faith.

Jude and 2 Peter

2 Peter is so different from 1 Peter that scholars think they should be discussed as having completely different settings. Conversely, the issues underlying Jude (and even some of Jude's language) are so similar to 2 Peter that teachers of the New Testament often discuss them together. Indeed, many scholars think that the author of 2 Peter drew on the very wording of Jude when writing 2 Peter 2:1-18 and 3:1-3.

The name "Jude" is a short form of "Judas," a brother of James and Jesus (Mark 6:3). However, scholars think that someone much later than the original Jude wrote in Jude's name. The book of 2 Peter was written in the form of a last will and testament.

In Jude, false teachers had once again come through the community. These traveling teachers taught that those who believed in Jesus were free from ethical restraints and free to do whatever they pleased (Jude 3-4, 8). For example, their sexual liberty knew no bounds (Jude 8, 16). A similar situation seems to be afoot in the church to which 2 Peter was addressed. People from outside the church brought "cleverly devised myths" into the community (2 Peter 1:16; 2:1-3, 12-22).

Jude warns the congregation that if they persist in such behavior, they will be condemned (Jude 14-23). Likewise, the author of 2 Peter reminds his readers that as God punished angels and people in previous generations, so God will also punish the ungodly in their own day (2 Peter 2:4-10). The book of 2 Peter ramps up this theme in 3:1-10, where the author pleads with readers to change their behavior because the day of the Lord Jesus' return and the final judgment are coming soon.

The Book of Revelation

I find that people have two different attitudes toward the book of Revelation. On the one hand, some people are mystified because the book of Revelation contains so many word-pictures that are foreign to us. "How can we make sense of this?" On the other hand, many people have been influenced by popular interpretations of the book of Revelation in the media and think that the book was written to inform people today that *we* are living in the last days. In my opinion, neither of these attitudes is correct. We can best understand what the book of Revelation is saying today if we grasp what it was saying to its own time. To understand the book of Revelation, we begin by recognizing that it was written by a visionary known to us only by the name of John around 90-95 C.E. At that time the churches in John's part of the world (around the Aegean Sea) were being harassed by the Roman Empire because the churches would not agree to worship Caesar. This brought them the condemnation of the Roman Empire. John was imprisoned on the island of Patmos (Revelation 1:9). He describes a series of visions. These are not relayed in linear time, but unfold like a spiral in which there is a general forward movement but in which the author circles back and revisits ideas already expressed.

John wrote Revelation because many in the seven churches he addressed were suffering, and some were in danger of leaving the church. Some were even considering rejoining the life and cult of the Roman Empire. John wanted to discourage these believers from abandoning their Christian faith.

John communicates these ideas through a series of word-pictures that would have made sense to his readers in antiquity even if they are difficult for us today. After revealing that the risen and ascended Christ is sovereign over the world (Revelation 1:12-20), the author points out how the churches to which he is writing are being unfaithful, and so he calls for repentance (Revelation 2:1–3:22). John then unfolds a spectacular vision of heaven to assure the congregation of God's absolute control (Revelation 4:1–5:14).

Revelation describes the opening of seven seals, the sort of seals that would have secured an official document at the time. As the author of Revelation pictures these seals being opened, he gives us a peek at what is sealed in each scroll. The secret that is now unsealed is that the turmoil within the empire is a sign that the end is near. The turmoil is also a part of the process by which God was destroying the empire. God will not complete the destruction of the empire nor bring about the Realm until the Second Coming of Jesus (Revelation 6:1–8:1). The book then describes a scene with seven trumpets. These pealing trumpets announce that the suffering of the empire will increase as the end of time draws near (Revelation 8:2–9:21). John reminds the churches that they will continue to suffer during this long process (Revelation 10:1–12:17). They must avoid participating in Roman religion, especially worship of Caesar (Revelation 13:1-18).

God will re-create heaven and earth in a new world order (or cosmos) in which the boundary between heaven and earth disappears and the Realm of God is in force in every individual life and in every social circumstance.

The churches need to pay special attention to John's message because the end-time destruction is upon them (Revelation 14:1–16:21). Using figurative language, John speaks of Rome as "the great whore of Babylon" and foresees a violent, bloody end for it (Revelation 17:1–19:21). After Rome is destroyed, God will consign Satan — here seen as the power behind Rome — and his minions to eternal punishment (Revelation 20:1-15). God will then re-create heaven and earth in a new world order (or cosmos) in which the boundary between heaven and earth disappears and the Realm of God is in force in every individual life and in every social circumstance. Truly, it will be a new heaven and new earth (Revelation 21:1–22:5). John shares this powerful vision to lure the community into being faithful during the painful transition from the old world into the new.

QUESTIONS FOR DISCUSSION

1. According to the book of Hebrews, the major goal of the Christian life is to leave this world and journey to the heavenly world. Is that what you also see as the major goal of a life of faith? If not, what do you see as that goal?

2. 1 Peter addresses the church as if it is a community of strangers, aliens, and exiles, implying that the church is not in the mainstream of culture but is an alternative to the dominant culture. This is a very popular way of speaking of the church today. If you are a member of a congregation, to what degree would you say your congregation is really an alternative community within North American society? To what degree is the church simply a mirror of that culture?

3. For Jude, the Christian community was compromised because members of the church were engaging in the same permissive behavior as the culture at large. Some people claim that a similar phenomenon is taking place today: Some churches are going along with permissive trends in the culture. Others say that, on some issues, the church is not more permissive but more progressive. How would you assess these two perspectives?

4. 2 Peter takes the form of a last will and testament in which the author lays out a body of teaching to be remembered after the writer's death. Think about your own testament. For what would you like to be remembered after your death?

5. The book of Revelation regards the Roman Empire as idolatrous, corrupt, exploitative, and violent. Some Christians today claim that the United States is similar to the Roman Empire. What do you think? John believed that God was destroying the empire. The churches to which John wrote could not change that process, but they could call people to repent of the error of cooperating with Rome. Do you think that is an adequate role for Christians today? Or should Christians try more actively to change the direction of our culture?

CHAPTER 11

Some Big Ideas in and around the New Testament

When I took chemistry, we learned that each element on the periodic table has its own integrity. The elements can be combined to make compounds that work together, but some combinations are dangerous, even explosive. In a lab session, I misread the instructions regarding the amount of acid I was supposed to put into a solution. When I combined the elements, they made a loud noise, boiled over, and splashed acid all over the laboratory table, creating a dangerous situation.

In a similar way, scholars urge us to follow the path we have taken in the last several chapters of focusing on the distinctive messages of different authors (such as Paul) or of different books (such as the Gospel of Mark) rather than to mesh them together so that the particular ideas from particular authors or books are blended. Mixing ideas across writers and books can distort and even destroy our perception of the unique message of a given writer.

We can be enriched, however, by comparing and contrasting the distinctive ideas in different authors and books. By doing so, we can also identify perceptions that authors have in common. When I want to know what the New Testament has to say about love, for example, I should study the authentic writings of Paul on that subject and then compare and contrast Paul's ideas with those found in the Gospel of John, 1 Peter, and other authors and texts.

In this chapter, I discuss several of the big ideas of a number of

New Testament authors.[1] I will call to your attention some of the distinctive emphases of particular authors or books. I also consider a few relevant big questions and issues not central to the New Testament itself but likely to come up when reading it. This chapter organizes these explorations in alphabetical order and is limited to one or two paragraphs per issue. Perhaps these limited forays will spark you to want to find out more.

As I get older, I speak less and less of *the* New Testament teaching on a particular subject. Instead, I seek to find ways to articulate the diversity of perspectives within the New Testament while acknowledging points that its authors may have in common.

A Shift in Perspective from Individual to Community and Cosmos

Several of the following comments are based on a shift in perspective that is taking place in our time. Christians have typically thought of the New Testament as being concerned first and foremost with the standing of the individual before God. Does God love me and will God save me? Or am I condemned?

However, in the past number of years, teachers of the New Testament have increasingly realized that people in the time of the New Testament were concerned not just about the individual's relationship with God but about the community of faith and the larger world. In their different ways, the New Testament authors seek to assure their faith communities that God is at work to provide security in their social world and in the natural world. Of course, in the Realm of God, individuals are fully accepted and loved. However, for

---

1. Many important ideas have already been discussed in this book and will not be repeated in the current chapter. Among them are ascension, Caesar, crucifixion, demons, destruction of the temple, devil (Satan), end-time thinking, gentiles, Holy Spirit, Jewish people, law (Torah), Lord's Supper, miracles (signs), Pentecost, Realm of God, repentance, resurrection, Roman occupation, second coming, two-story universe (John), and Word (as a designation for Jesus).

the New Testament writers in continuity with early Jewish concern, God's blessing will encompass both humankind and all of nature.

Communal Identity

In North America, we often think of identity as a matter of who we are as individuals. Yes, we live in networks of relationships (for example, households and congregations), but we think of ourselves as individual operators. In contrast, people in antiquity perceived their identity communally. An individual did not just belong to a community but embodied the community. The power and mission of the community flowed through the individual. When the individual acted, the group acted through that person.

People in antiquity perceived their identity communally. An individual did not just belong to a community but embodied the community.

The writings of the New Testament are not directed toward individuals but toward congregations as communities whose members were inherently connected. When individuals violate the identity of the community, the community cannot be what it was intended to be. The books of the New Testament were not written merely to speak to individual behavior but to help the congregations recover their sense of identity. The clearest instance of this phenomenon in the New Testament is Paul referring to the church as the "body of Christ" (for example, Romans 12:4-5; 1 Corinthians 12:12-31). The members of the congregation are connected organically in the same way that the parts of a human body are related. The Gospel of John uses the image of Jesus being the vine and the congregation being the branches to describe this shared identity (John 15:1-17).

Faith

Christians often make the innocent mistake of saying, "We are saved by faith." The actual New Testament statement is that we are "saved by grace through faith" (based on Ephesians 2:8). Faith does not save. God's grace saves people. In both the Old Testament and the New Testament, faith amounts to believing that God is doing and will do what God promises. Moreover, in both Testaments, having real faith always elicits behavior that shows that a person or community truly trusts in God's paths. To have faith is not simply to agree in mind and heart with a body of ideas but to live faithfully.

With this understanding in mind, some scholars are looking at passages that have been understood as speaking about human faith and coming to the conclusion that they might instead be referring to God's faithfulness. For instance, many scholars now agree that Romans 1:17 can be read, "The one who is righteous will live [that is, be welcomed into the Realm of God] on the basis of God's faithfulness." Scholars further agree that some places in the New Testament that use the phrase "faith in Jesus Christ" could better be understood as referring to "the faithfulness of Jesus Christ" (for example, Romans 3:22). If this is correct, it adds up to the idea that it is God who brings us into his Realm and not our own fluctuating faith.

> **To have faith is not simply to agree in mind and heart with a body of ideas but to live faithfully.**

Hebrews puts forward a distinctive understanding of faith that goes along with its two-story view of the cosmos (see p. 130). Faith is "the assurance of things hoped for, the conviction of things not seen" (Heb. 11:1). Faith is believing that a person will journey from the present world (the first story) to heaven (the second story).

Grace

A favorite hymn of many Christian communities deeply expresses one foundational theme of North American churches: "Amazing grace, how sweet the sound, that saved a wretch like me."[2] The word

2. John Newton, "Amazing Grace," in *Chalice Hymnal,* ed. Daniel B. Merrick (St. Louis: Chalice Press, 1995), no. 546.

"grace" means "unmerited favor" or receiving good things, like the love of God, even if you don't deserve them. When we say, "Jesus saves us as an act of grace," we mean that we do not deserve to be saved but Jesus acts on our behalf as an act of generous love.

Christians sometimes think that Jesus was the first person to show grace and that there was no grace before him. However, the notion of grace is found in the Old Testament to describe God's relationship with Israel and with some of Israel's ancestors (for example, Genesis 6:8; Exodus 33:12, 19; 34:6-7; Deuteronomy 7:7-8; Psalm 4:1; Jeremiah 31:2). Israel did not earn God's favor but received that favor as God's free and unmerited act of love. In the New Testament, more than 90 percent of the uses of the word "grace" occur in Paul's writings. Although the idea of grace is part of the backdrop of the Gospels and Acts, the actual language of grace is very rarely found there. For Paul, Christ is the way the grace that God poured out on Israel is shared with gentiles.

People sometimes speak of "free grace." However, the word "free" is not necessary because grace is always "free." Grace and mercy are intertwined (see below).

Titles for Jesus

The name of the central human figure of the New Testament is "Jesus," which translates the Hebrew name "Joshua." As pointed out earlier, the Hebrew name Joshua means "God saves." In addition to speaking of Jesus by name, the New Testament writers use a number of titles for Jesus that express the meaning of his life

God anointed Jesus to bring in the Realm through all he did, in his preaching, teaching, working miracles, suffering, resurrection, ascension, and his eventual coming again.

and ministry. The designation "Jesus Christ," for instance, means "Jesus is the Christ."

Christ. Another way to translate the word "Christ" is "Messiah." The word "Christ" or "messiah" means "anointed one" and refers to the Jewish practice of appointing leaders by anointing them with oil (for example, 2 Samuel 19:21; Isaiah 45:1). Christians sometimes casually talk about *the* Jewish view of the messiah. However, the Jewish people at the time of Jesus had several different ideas of what the messiah might be. An important topic of conversation in the Judaism of Jesus' day was: "Will there be a messiah (a Christ) and, if so, what will the messiah be like?" Calling Jesus "messiah" is one of the church's ways of entering that conversation and stating that Jesus was God's messiah. God anointed Jesus to bring in the Realm through all he did, in his preaching, teaching, working miracles, suffering, resurrection, ascension, and his eventual coming again.

Lord. This title can be confusing to people today who remember that the Old Testament often refers to God as "Lord." This use of "Lord" also occurs in the New Testament (as in Romans 11:34 and Mark 13:20). However, at the time of Jesus the word "lord" could be used of many figures who had authority over a specific sphere of life. To call Jesus "lord" was not immediately to equate him with God but to indicate that he was a ruler in life's affairs. In Roman culture, Caesar was sometimes called "lord." From the point of view of Jesus' followers, not only was the lordship of Jesus superior to that of Caesar, but Caesar himself would one day have to answer to Jesus.

Son of Man. This title and the next are among the most confusing to readers today. The title "Son of Man" sounds like a reference to the humanity of Jesus. However, this title derives from Daniel 7:13-14, where it refers to the end-time redeemer and judge, a representative of God whom God would send from heaven. When the New Testament writers call Jesus "Son of Man," they indicate that the end-time figure was already present in the world in a provisional way in the person of Jesus.

Son of God. This designation, too, had a different first-century meaning from the one that comes to mind to many people today. We tend to think that it refers to Jesus' divinity. However, its New Testament usage comes from Psalm 2:7. Israel sang this when the prince was being elevated to be king. At the time of the coronation, God adopted the king as God's own son. In ancient culture, that meant that the son would inherit the purposes and power of the parent. Son of God is a first-century way of saying that God adopted Jesus to continue God's purposes. Indeed, God empowered Jesus to do so.

Mercy

One of my uncles was a judge. He reported that from time to time a person appearing for sentencing would request "the mercy of the court." Such people know that they deserve punishment, but they hope that the court will not give them the full punishment they deserve. While this idea is included in the biblical notion of mercy, the biblical concept of mercy is broader and deeper.

The main Hebrew word behind the Greek word for "mercy" in the New Testament is a word that refers to a profound and unshakable love and is sometimes translated "steadfast love," "lovingkindness," or "covenantal loyalty." Scholars often say that this word is *the* most important concept in the Old Testament when it comes to describing God's relationship with his people. God has made a promise (covenant) with Israel. God shows utterly unshakable love toward Israel (for example, Exodus 34:6-7; Deuteronomy 5:10; Psalms 98:3; 100:5; Isaiah 54:8). Another Hebrew word that is also translated "mercy" in the New Testament carries the idea of profound compassion (for example, Deuteronomy 13:17; Isaiah 54:7; Hosea 2:19).

When the New Testament speaks of God's mercy toward Israel, it not only refers to God's covenant faithfulness to Israel but assumes that that faithfulness still endures (for example, Romans 9:15, 23; 11:30-31). When New Testament writers speak of God's mercy flowing through Jesus, they mean that the covenant loyalty that God displayed toward Israel is now also expressed toward the followers of Jesus, including gentiles (for example, Romans 11:30-31; 1 Peter 1:3; 2:10). Jesus' disciples are to show similar covenant faithfulness (for example, Matthew 5:7; 18:33) to each other and to God.

Predestination (Election)

In Bible studies in local congregations, I am often asked whether the New Testament teaches some form of election or predestination. In some churches, the idea that God chooses who will find salvation or enter the Realm is foundational. However, North Americans accustomed to self-determination are often uneasy with such an idea. Moreover, they are afraid that they might not be among those who are predestined for salvation.

Some documents in the New Testament do teach some form of predestination, such as Romans 8:28-30; 9:10-13; 11:2; Ephesians 1:3-14; and 2 Timothy 1:9. The idea of predestination came into the New Testament from Jewish thinking about the end of time. As we discussed in Chapters 2, 3, and 4, writers in antiquity concerned with the end of time perceived that the world was in chaos. In order to nourish hope, they reasoned that God had predetermined how history would unfold. Their idea of election focused not on the salvation of individuals but on God's control of history. This message was meant to instill confidence for living out the faith. The language of predestination is thus intended to assure the congregation that even in the face of difficult circumstances, God is working in the world. The congregation may find itself in such a bad way that they are tempted to believe that God has abandoned them. The idea of election is a way of saying, "No matter how bad things look to you now, you can have the confidence that long ago God decided to act for your benefit and blessing."

From the New Testament perspective, the fundamental issue is not who is included in God's circle and who is not included. Over the years, some people in the church have become distracted from their main purpose by wondering, "Who is in and who is out?" The foundational purpose of the notion of election is to assure those who have embraced the living God and committed themselves to live faithfully through the church that they can count on God's providence now and in the future.

Salvation: Limited or Universal?

Many people are vexed by the issue of whether only a limited number of people will be saved (exclusive salvation) or whether all people will be saved (universal salvation). Whereas people today do not often pause long enough to define what they mean by salvation, the New Testament does have clear notions about salvation. As we noted in Chapter 4, in the New Testament "salvation" means that one has a place in the coming Realm of God (end-time thinking) or that one will make the journey from the world into heaven (John and Hebrews). Those who believe that God saves through Jesus may experience aspects of salvation already.

Christian people often try to find texts in the New Testament (and throughout the Bible) that support each side. In this endeavor, those who advocate limited salvation have more support because the New Testament contains many texts that teach limited salvation (for example, Matthew 25:31-46; John 3:16-21; 1 Corinthians 1:18; Revelation 20:7-15). The New Testament does contain occasional passages that can be read as supporting universal salvation (for example, Ephesians 1:9-10). Those who make the case for universal salvation do so not only by quoting biblical passages that seem to suggest universal salvation, but must argue that the very nature of God calls for universal salvation.[3]

Sin

In the Old Testament the idea of "sin" can be expressed as missing the goal (or the mark) that God had for his people (the analogy might be running in the wrong direction from the finish line). In particular it referred to violating or transgressing the covenant bond that God made with Israel. Sin was not so much a deep alienation from God

3. For example, contemporary writers moving in this stream include Rob Bell, *Love Wins: A Book about Heaven, Hell and the Fate of Every Person Who Ever Lived* (New York: HarperOne, 2011), and Phillip Gulley and James Mulholland, *If Grace Is True: Why God Will Save Every Person* (New York: HarperCollins, 2004).

as failing to follow the path that God intended for blessing his people. The Old Testament says that God gave the people of Israel rites to be practiced in the temple to bring about forgiveness and guidelines for making restitution. These were to liberate individuals and communities from the burden of the sins they committed so that they could begin anew. The story of the fall in Genesis 3 (see pp. 19, 56) was often taken to mean that the world could never be sin-free and that people were born into a world that offered endless opportunities to sin. However, in the Old Testament world, there was no notion that people were born with inherent guilt. People would feel personal guilt as a result of committing specific sins.

New Testament writers employed these ideas. Sin could include acting against God's intentions for the human community (for example, 1 Corinthians 6:18). In these cases, forgiveness had much the same meaning as in the Old Testament. The New Testament writers seem particularly aghast at flagrant acts of gentile sin such as idolatry, exploiting others, failing to care for one another, and violence. For gentiles, according to Paul, the death of Jesus functioned much like Jewish rites of forgiveness in the Old Testament. The death of Jesus could release gentiles from the burden of sin (for example, Romans 3:24-26). In addition, since Paul, like many of his Jewish contemporaries, looked at the world as in the throes of the end of time, Paul viewed sin not simply as a human action but as a power that enslaved people (Romans 5:12-13). Release from the power of sin would be complete in the coming of the Realm when God destroyed the power of sin (Romans 6:22-23). New Testament writers who use the word "sinner" usually have in mind a person who has flagrantly disobeyed (for example, Matthew 11:19). Whenever you come across the word "sin" in the New Testament, you need to figure out how that word is being used in the passage you're looking at.

QUESTIONS FOR DISCUSSION

1. As you read through this chapter, did any of the ideas catch you by surprise? If so, which ones? What were the surprises?

2. Do you think of your congregation more as a collection of individuals or as a real community? How would it change your perception and behavior to see it as community?

3. Consider two possible translations of Romans 3:22 in view of the meanings of faith as to human trust or faithful activity. (a) "The righteousness of God [has been revealed] through faith in Jesus Christ for all who believe." (b) "The righteousness of God [has been revealed] through the faithfulness of Jesus Christ for all who believe." What is the difference in meaning? Which makes more sense to you?

4. We may think generally of two views of sin in the New Testament: (1) Sin as transgressing God's desires for the world; (2) Sin as a power that enslaves. Can you identify examples of each from your own world?

5. What difference would it make in both your thinking and behavior to believe in limited salvation? To believe in universal salvation?

CHAPTER 12

Some of the Most Famous Passages in the New Testament

Some passages in the New Testament are so well known that Christians refer to them by short phrases such as "John Three Sixteen" or "The Love Chapter." A few passages have even made their way into channels of mainstream culture in North America. Even if you have never read the New Testament, I'll bet you have heard someone say, "She was a good Samaritan" or "He is really a prodigal." If you are a Christian, being aware of these designations can help you dialogue more easily with other Christians and can deepen your appreciation of the Bible as sacred Scripture. If you are interested in the New Testament as literature, knowing a little bit about these passages can help you appreciate some of the biblical literary backdrop of our culture.

This chapter discusses ten of the most well-known passages from the New Testament. I give the passage either in whole or in part, and then comment briefly on the meaning of the passage in its historical and literary settings. In the interests of brevity, I summarize the content of parts of some of the longer passages.

Let me caution readers. While it may be handy to use abbreviated titles such as "The Faith Chapter," a serious student of the Bible will try to look closely at the passage itself and not simply consider its nickname a complete summary of its meaning. The popular designation of the passage never captures the fullness of the passage itself.

John Three Sixteen: John 3:16

"For God so loved the world that he gave his only Son, so that everyone who believes in him may not perish but have eternal life."

Box 20. John 3:16

John 3:16 is so well known that the words "John 3:16" or "John Three Sixteen" often appear by themselves on tee shirts, on posters, and in many other forms.

Christians are drawn to this text because it clearly affirms God's love for the world. The word "world" here refers to the writer's negative understanding of that place which is dark, false, and full of hate and violence (p. 115). Christians sometimes fail to note that John 3:16-17 is followed by the more narrow view of love in John 3:18. "Those who believe in him [Jesus] are not condemned; but those who do not believe in him are condemned already."

The Love Chapter: 1 Corinthians 13

"If I speak in the tongues of mortals [of men] and of angels, but do not have love, I am a noisy gong or a clanging cymbal . . . Love is patient; love is kind; love is not envious or boastful or arrogant or rude. . . . Love never ends. But as for prophecies, they will come to an end; as for tongues, they will cease. . . . When I was a child, I spoke like a child, I reasoned like a child; when I became an adult, I put an end to childish ways. For now we see in a mirror, dimly, but then we will see face to face. . . . And now faith, hope, and love abide, these three; and the greatest of these is love." (1 Corinthians 13:1-13)

Box 21. The Love Chapter

1 Corinthians 13, often called "the love chapter," is often used at marriage ceremonies and holy unions.

Paul here is giving guidance on how to handle a real nitty-gritty conflict in the congregation (1 Corinthians 12:1–14:40). Some church members claimed that speaking in tongues and other dramatic gifts were more important than other gifts. For Paul, the Spirit gives varieties of gifts to build up the one body, or congregation. Love, in this setting, is not just an emotion but is actively working for the good of others, especially for the community. Love is the most important spiritual gift.

The Golden Rule: Matthew 7:12

"In everything, do to others as you would have them do to you." (Matthew 7:12)

Box 22. The Golden Rule

Jesus was not the first Jewish leader to summarize the heart of Judaism in the golden rule. Several others did so about the same time. Perhaps the most memorable is this story. A gentile considering converting to Judaism asked Rabbi Hillel (who lived about the same time as Jesus) to summarize the Torah while the gentile stood on one foot. Hillel replied, "What is hateful to your fellow, don't do." Hillel continued, "That's the entirety of the Torah, everything else is elaboration."*

* *Shabbat* 31A, in Jacob Neusner, *The Babylonian Talmud: A Translation and Commentary* (Peabody, Mass.: Hendrickson, 2005), vol. 2, p. 127.

We often hear the golden rule used as a general life principle. However, in its context in the Sermon on the Mount, another famous passage (Matthew 5:1–7:29), it challenges Matthew's congregation to live in the world in ways that are shaped by the Realm of God and so relate to other people using the principles of the Realm of God peppered throughout the larger sermon.

The Lord's Prayer: Matthew 6:9–13

> "Our Father in heaven, hallowed be your name. Your kingdom [Realm] come. Your will be done, on earth as it is in heaven. Give us this day our daily bread. And forgive us our debts as we also have forgiven our debtors. And do not bring us to the time of trial, but rescue us from the evil one." (Matthew 6:9-13)

Box 23. The Lord's Prayer

Many Christian congregations pray the Lord's Prayer every Sunday morning, concluding, "For yours (thine) is the kingdom (Realm), the power, and the glory forever." However, that conclusion is not found in the best ancient manuscripts of the New Testament.

This prayer is a plea for God to bring in the Realm. Each line refers to an aspect of the Realm of God. Some translations have "And forgive us our trespasses" or "forgive us our sins" instead of "forgive us our debts" (Matthew 6:12). "Debts" is the best translation because the Realm includes release from financial debts as well as other violations of relationship (trespasses, sins).

The Faith Chapter: Hebrews 11:1-40

"Now faith is the assurance of things hoped for, the conviction of things not seen. . . . By faith Abraham obeyed God when [Abraham] was called to set out for a place that he was to receive as an inheritance; and he set out, not knowing where he was going." (Hebrews 11:1, 8).

> **Box 24. The Faith Chapter**
>
> The "faith chapter" recounts a long list of people from the Jewish tradition who lived in faith — that is, in the expectation of reaching heaven or being made perfect — but who "did not receive what was promised." For Hebrews, only Jesus makes access to heaven possible.

In this passage, the "things hoped for . . . the things not seen" are the heavenly world. Faith is living in the confidence that one is on the journey from earth to heaven. This view of faith is only one of several understandings in the New Testament (see pp. 143-44). Readers need to respect the particular definitions of faith in each biblical writer.

The Good Samaritan: Luke 10:29-37

"A man was going down from Jerusalem to Jericho, and fell into the hands of robbers, who stripped him, beat him, and went away, leaving him half dead. Now by chance a priest was going down that road; and when he saw him, he passed by on the other side. So likewise a Levite. . . . But a Samaritan while traveling came near him; and when he saw him, he was moved with pity. He went to him and bandaged his wounds [and] brought him to an inn. . . . Which of these three, do you think, was a neighbor to the [one] who fell into the hands of the robbers?" [One of Jesus'

hearers] said, "The one who showed . . . mercy." Jesus said . . . ,
"Go and do likewise." (Luke 10:29-37)

Box 25. The Parable of the Good Samaritan

The church has sometimes turned the parable of the Good Samaritan
into an allegory in which the man by the side of the road represented
Adam who fell into sin. The priest and the Levite represented Judaism
in its inability to help the sinner. The Good Samaritan is Christ. However, nothing in the parable itself or in the Gospel of Luke authorizes
such allegorical interpretation.

When we call someone a "good Samaritan," we usually mean a
helpful person. Luke had more in mind in telling this parable. Samaritans were often looked down on. Luke uses the Samaritan as
the hero to help the church recognize that those looked down upon
can be faithful models of how God wants people to live. Samaritans
are welcome in the Realm of God. Even more broadly, the Samaritan
stands for anyone the church might encounter who is an outsider,
an other.

The Prodigal Son: Luke 15:11-32

"There was a man who had two sons. The younger of them said
to his father, 'Father, give me the share of the property that will
belong to me.'" So the father divided the property, and the younger son went to a far country, where he squandered everything
and began living with pigs. "But when he came to himself he
said, 'I will get up and go to my father, and I will say to him, "Father, I have sinned against heaven and before you; I am no longer worthy to be called your son; treat me like one of your hired
hands."'" However, upon seeing him from a distance, the father
ran to him, embraced him, and declared, "Quickly, bring out a

robe . . . and put it on him; put a ring on his finger. . . . And get the fatted calf and kill it; . . . for this son of mine was dead and is alive again."

However, the elder son was not at home when this reunion occurred. He was in a field working, and when he discovered the preparations for the feast, "he became angry and refused to go in." The father came to the elder brother in the field and pleaded with him to come in, but the elder boy refused. "I have never disobeyed your command; yet you have never given me even a young goat so that I might celebrate with my friends." The father concludes, "Son, you are always with me, and all that is mine is yours. But we had to celebrate." (Luke 15:11-32)

Box 26. The Prodigal Son

The church has often focused only on the prodigal and used the parable as an invitation to people who have acted in prodigal ways to believe that God welcomes them in the same way that the father welcomed the younger child. Luke wanted his readers also to identify with the elder child and to recognize ways that they resented and resisted prodigals coming into the church.

Although this story is known as "the prodigal son," it is really the story of a father and two children. Although the characters are Jewish, the younger (prodigal) son essentially becomes a gentile when he behaves in a decadent way and winds up living with swine. When he repents and returns home, the father welcomes him. This welcome both assures prodigals that they have a place in the Realm of God when they repent and challenges Luke's congregation to welcome all who repent (including gentiles). The older son (the elder brother) resents the welcome given to the younger. As the parable ends, the older child is standing in the field. We do not know whether or not he will join the celebration in the house. The parable forces Luke's congregation to ask, "Will we be like the older brother, and resist the welcome that God has given to prodigals, or will we join the celebration going on in the Realm of God?"

The Great Commandment: Mark 12:28-34

"The first [commandment] is, 'Hear, O Israel: the Lord our God, the Lord is one; you shall love the Lord your God with all your heart, and with all your soul, and with all your mind, and with all your strength.' The second is this, 'You shall love your neighbor as yourself.' There is no other commandment greater than these." (Mark 12:29-31)

Box 27. The Great Commandment

This passage has parallels in Matthew 22:34-40 and in Luke 10:25-28. As a little detective work, look for differences in the three accounts, including differences in wording and in literary context.

This passage helps answer an important question that emerged in Judaism (even among Jesus' followers) after the Romans destroyed the temple in 70 C.E. What did it mean to be Jewish when the community could no longer carry out the sacrificial rites at the temple? The answer: The essence of being Jewish is loving God and neighbor.

In My Father's House Are Many Rooms: John 14:1-3

"Do not let your hearts be troubled. Believe in God, believe also in me. In my Father's house there are many dwelling places [rooms, mansions]. If it were not so, would I have told you that I go to prepare a place for you? And if I go and prepare a place for you, I will come again and will take you to myself, so that where I am, there you may be also." (John 14:1-3)

Box 28. God's House Has Many Rooms

According to the Gospel of John, only those who believe in Jesus have a place in heaven. "I am the way, the truth, and the life. No one comes to the Father except through me" (John 14:6).

This passage was a call to endurance to the members of John's congregation who were suffering in the world. The text promises that they will follow Jesus to God's home in heaven where Jesus has prepared rooms, dwelling places, to welcome them.

The Beatitudes: Matthew 5:1-12

"Blessed are the poor in spirit, for theirs is the kingdom [Realm] of heaven. . . . Blessed are the meek, for they will inherit the earth. . . . Blessed are the peacemakers, for they will be called children of God. Blessed are those who are persecuted for righteousness' sake, for theirs is the kingdom [Realm] of heaven." (Matthew 5:3-10)

Box 29. The Beatitudes

Note that the beatitudes are not commands: "You *must* become poor in spirit." They are promises. Those who are poor in spirit *are* part of the community of the Realm of God.

In the beatitudes, to be "blessed" is not simply to be happy or fortunate but to be included in the Realm of God. Those persecuted for righteousness' sake, for instance, are not happy in a conventional sense but are "blessed" because they have a place in the coming Realm of God.

I Pray That They May All Be One: John 17:1-26

"I ask not only on behalf of these, but also on behalf of those who will believe in me through their word, that they may all be one. As you, Father, are in me and I am in you, may they also be in us, so that the world may believe that you have sent me." (John 17:20-21)

Box 30. That They May All Be One

John 17 with its call to be one is a favorite passage in the contemporary ecumenical movement — a movement that tries to draw the many different Christian denominations and movements into closer relationships with one another.

Scholars refer to John 17 as Jesus' "High-Priestly Prayer" because Jesus prayed like a priest before God for his followers to be "one." That oneness was important at the time of the Gospel of John. As we saw in Chapter 8, the community to which John wrote was alienated from the traditional synagogue. Because a person's identity in antiquity was communal, the congregation of the Gospel of John needed to know that they were "one," that is, a real community of support for one another in the midst of challenges to their identity.

The New Heaven and the New Earth: Revelation 21:1-22:5

"I saw the holy city, the New Jerusalem, coming down out of heaven from God, prepared as a bride adorned for her husband. . . . '[God] will wipe away every tear from their eyes.' . . . The city lies foursquare. . . . and the street of the city is pure gold, transparent as glass. . . . On either side of the river is the tree of life with its twelve kinds of fruit . . . and the leaves of the tree are for the healing of the nations. . . . And there will be no more night." (Revelation 21:2, 4, 16, 21; 22:2, 5)

Box 31. New Heaven and New Earth

While the new heaven and the new earth of Revelation 21 and 22 will come fully only in the future, the vision of community in these chapters is meant for the present. The vision of community in this passage is a standard that ought to help us evaluate how well the church is being that community. Its vision can even inform how we look at all other types of community (including cities, states, and nations).

Chapters 21 and 22 of the book of Revelation give a lengthy, detailed description of a city called the "New Jerusalem." Christians sometimes think that these chapters refer to heaven as a place where people go after death. In the book of Revelation, however, they describe the Realm of God, the coming time when God will destroy the barrier between heaven and earth and when all that will be included in the final Realm will be together forever in one new community.

Of course, being able to quote a passage of Scripture or to find a passage in the Bible are not ends in themselves. But Scripture is a fundamental resource for the Christian life. Being familiar with passages from the Bible — and being able to find them — can be wonderful helps when life is difficult and when entering into conversation about important matters through all the seasons of life.

Box 32. Some Other Well-Known Texts

Of course, there are many other passages that are well known in Christian circles. I list a few here by referring to key lines or phrases.

"A wise [person] built [a] house on rock. . . . a foolish [person] built [a] house on sand" (Matthew 7:24, 26).

"All have sinned and fall short of the glory of God" (Romans 3:23).

"As you did it to one of the least of these, . . . you did it to me" (Matthew 25:40).

"By grace you have been saved through faith" (Ephesians 2:8).

"Unless I see the mark of the nails in his hands, . . . I will not believe" [Doubting Thomas] (John 20:24-29).

Forgive "not seven times . . . but seventy-seven times" (Matthew 18:22)

"I am the bread of life" (John 6:35) . . . "the good shepherd" (John 10:11) . . . "the light of the world" (John 8:12) . . . the resurrection and the life" (John 11:25) . . . "I am the vine, you are the branches" (John 15:5).

"I give you a new commandment, that you love one another" (John 13:34).

"If anyone is in Christ, there is a new creation" (2 Corinthians 5:17).

"In Christ God was reconciling the world to himself (2 Corinthians 5:19).

"In the beginning was the Word, and the Word was with God" (John 1:1).

"Go . . . and make disciples of all nations, baptizing them" (Matthew 28:19).

Sermon on the Mount (Matthew 5:1–7:29)

The lost sheep (Matthew 18:10-14; Luke 15:3-7)

"The fruit of the Spirit is love, joy, peace, patience, kindness . . ." (Galatians 5:22).

"The Spirit of the Lord is upon me . . . to bring good news to the poor" (Luke 4:18).

"This is my body; . . . this is my blood" (Matt. 26:26-30; 1 Corinthians 11:23-25).

Shepherds visit the infant Jesus at his birth (Luke 2:8-20).

"You cannot serve God and wealth [mammon]" (Matthew 6:24).

Virginal conception and birth of Jesus (Matt. 1:18-25; Luke 1:26-38; 2:1-7)

Wise men (three kings, astrologers) visit the infant Jesus (Matthew 2:1-12).

QUESTIONS FOR DISCUSSION

1. Which of the texts above did you immediately recognize? Did your previous understanding of the texts go along with the brief explanations that followed?

2. Which of the above passages seem(s) the most meaningful to you at this juncture of your life? How does that passage speak to you? Perhaps you could commit it to memory.

3. Do you recollect a passage you think is from the New Testament but is not in these lists? Even if you cannot remember a word or a phrase, look for it in a concordance (see Appendix B, pp. 182-85). If the passage is not in the Bible, you've learned something important. For example, some people think that the Bible says, "God helps those who help themselves." But that saying does not occur in the Bible.

4. It is helpful and nurturing to the Christian life to be able to bring such passages to mind. Make a set of flash cards with the text of a passage on one side and the references to the book, chapter, and verses on the other. Practice identifying the passages by yourself or with a partner.

CHAPTER 13

Using the New Testament
in the Church Today

As the chapter title indicates, this chapter focuses on using the New Testament in the church today. If you are an active believer, you may have a natural interest in this chapter. If you are reading this volume simply to get background information about the New Testament, you might still be interested in this chapter because of the window it opens into the issues associated with the Bible in Christian communities. In either case, this chapter should help you understand why today's Christian communities sometimes come to quite different conclusions regarding what to believe and do.

The previous chapters have provided information about the content of the New Testament — major characters, big story lines, key events, important ideas, and multiple books. However, knowing what is inside the New Testament is not the same as knowing how the New Testament can help inform your own faith and behavior. How do you move from then to now, from valuable data about the New Testament in the ancient world to how to use that data when deciding what to believe and do today?

In the following, I describe two ways of understanding and using the New Testament in the church today. The heart of the chapter explores these two approaches with an eye toward their practical outcomes. The chapter concludes by asking you to think about your own place on the spectrum of interpretation.

Two Ways of Using the New Testament in the Church Today: Multiple Voice and Single Voice

For the church, a major goal of studying the New Testament is to determine how the New Testament can help us come to a compelling interpretation of God and of God's purposes for the church and the world. Toward this end, Christians use the New Testament in one of two basic ways.

Speaking of *two* basic ways of understanding the New Testament is an oversimplification. We might think instead of a spectrum of interpretations with these two perspectives as poles at either end. Most individuals and congregations fall somewhere between the poles. Many combinations and fine nuances are possible as you approach reading the New Testament this way. However, for discussion purposes, this oversimplification helps us see why different communities understand the New Testament differently.

I refer to one way of reading the New Testament as *multiple voices in conversation*. This perspective understands the New Testament to consist of multiple voices. The church brings the voices in the New Testament into conversation with many other voices in the world today in order to articulate how we understand the divine aims for us and for the world. *Reading the New Testament for the First Time* is written from this perspective. Since the voices in the conversation sometimes disagree with one another, we have to decide which ones are more persuasive.

I refer to the other way of using the New Testament as a *single voice speaking authoritatively*. From this point of view the New Testament speaks with a single unified voice. When the church understands the New Testament, the church understands God's aims. Of course, we have to clarify those aims and apply them.

Similarities and Differences in the Two Perspectives

These two ways of making sense of the New Testament for today share common convictions. Both groups believe in the existence of

God. While neither group thinks that we can know God fully, they do believe that we can know something of God's purposes. They share the notion that when human beings respond faithfully to God's purposes, the world has a better chance of being the kind of place God wants, and that when we do not respond faithfully to God's intentions, the world is less than it could be.

With respect to the New Testament, both approaches consider the interpreter's first responsibility to be to clarify what a passage from the New Testament meant to its audience in antiquity. Both groups insist that today's student of the Bible must respect how people in the world of antiquity would have understood the text. Insofar as possible, contemporary interpreters should avoid reading our own issues and values and behaviors into the ancient text. Let the New Testament speak in its own distinct words.

People at opposite ends of the spectrum of interpretation differ with one another in how they discern or figure out God's purposes for themselves and for the world. While both groups regard the New Testament as an important source, the multiple-voice group draws on a variety of sources in addition to the Bible in the process of understanding what God is about. These two camps have different views as to the inherent authority of the New Testament. They perceive God's role in the creation of the New Testament differently. Such key points of similarity and difference are summarized in Box 33 and developed in the next sections of the chapter.

The different groups sometimes come to quite different conclusions regarding the content of their understanding of God's purposes and about what human beings should do in response to those purposes. Sometimes people within each group arrive at points of view that are different from one another since different Bible readers can interpret the same data in different ways. The key word is "interpretation."

Box 33. Comparison of Two Views of Understanding and Using the New Testament

	Multiple-Voice Conversation	Single-Voice Authority
Sources of authority to which the church turns when discerning God's presence and purposes	The New Testament, the tradition of the church, experience, and reason	The New Testament is the most important authority.
Who wrote the New Testament?	Human beings	God through human beings
What does the New Testament contain?	Human words interpreting God's purposes	God's own words (or words with slight interpretation)
Relationship of different parts of the New Testament	The New Testament is a library with different authors offering their own perspectives.	All parts of the New Testament are internally consistent with one another.
Range of validity and applicability	The New Testament was written in and to specific cultural contexts; the church must assess the degree to which New Testament texts speak to other contexts.	The New Testament is universally valid in every time and place.
Role of the interpreting community	The community clarifies the meaning of the New Testament in its historical context and sets in motion a conversation to clarify how the New Testament might help the church today discern God's purposes.	To clarify the meaning of the New Testament in its historical context and apply it to today

How does the community evaluate and make use of the history of tradition after the Bible?	The community listens to the multiple voices in the tradition and brings them into dialogue with the New Testament (and with experience and reason) to determine points at which the tradition may have insight that the New Testament itself does not have and points at which tradition founders.	The community honors tradition when tradition agrees with the Bible or amplifies it in ways consistent with the New Testament itself, and the community criticizes tradition when tradition does not agree with the Bible.
How does the community evaluate and make use of experience?	The community believes that God is present and can be known in every moment; experience can alert us to the divine presence and purposes; consequently the community pays attention to the possibility that experience itself might be a source of awareness of God's presence and purposes.	When the experience of people today agrees with the New Testament, the community considers it valid experience, but when the experience of the community contradicts the experience of the New Testament, then the community needs to change its experience.
How does the community evaluate and make use of reason?	Reason is foundational to helping the conversation involving the Bible, tradition, and experience move toward ascertaining God's aims; reason (especially as expressed through science) can also be a source of perception regarding God's presence and purposes.	Reason can help the community extend the insights of the New Testament into fresh situations and can help the church establish the truth of the New Testament; however, when reason contradicts the New Testament, then reason must yield to the New Testament.

First Way: Multiple Voices in Conversation with Other Authorities

People who bring multiple voices into conversation with one another as a way of discovering God's presence and purposes typically listen to the voices of the New Testament, the tradition of the church, their own experience (and that of others), and reason.

From this perspective, the Bible was written by human beings who sought to interpret God's presence and guidance to particular communities. This understanding presupposes that God did not write the New Testament. The New Testament is a human interpretation of God's purposes. Over the years, the church has found that many insights in the New Testament provide trustworthy guidance.

I have already used the word "library" to describe the New Testament. While the different New Testament authors share common convictions, they each present slightly different nuances to these convictions. New Testament readers should bring different texts in the New Testament into dialogue with one another to help them discern divine wisdom.

Congregations and individuals at this end of the spectrum also listen to the multiple voices in Christian tradition, that is, Christian voices outside the Bible. The post–New Testament Christian tradition extends from the late first century C.E. to the present. It includes voices that can be quite different from each other. Christians attend to this broad tradition for insights that may not be present in the New Testament. This act of listening for insights from the tradition can help discern God's purposes on points regarding which the New Testament may be silent.

Churches of this type will also pay attention to experience as a resource for helping us identify God's aims. By experience, I mean everything that happens to us, including thoughts, actions, and feelings. Since God is present at every moment, a person can become aware of that presence in any circumstance. Given the fact that all experience occurs within culture, we must consider the possibility that the cultural lenses of earlier generations may have caused them to misperceive some of God's intentions. Fresh experience can lead to fresh insight. Of course, we must recognize that *our* experiences are also bounded by our cultural situations and may also cause us to misperceive.

Reason functions as a voice in this conversation in two ways. First, Christians seek logical consistency in the way in which they bring together the New Testament voices, tradition, and experience. They seek to avoid contradiction. Second, most of the understandings of the world that have currency today are informed by science. Christians in this camp seek an interpretation of God's purposes that is at home in the contemporary scientific world. This instinct is tempered by the recognition that the scientific worldview is not absolute and is always being revised.

This approach brings these different voices into conversation with one another. The Bible often plays the most important role, but not an imperial one. The key question is simply: "Based on our best listening to the New Testament, tradition, experience, and reason, what understandings of God's purposes make the most sense for our moment in history?"

Strengths and Weaknesses

The great strength of this approach is that it encourages the church to understand God's purposes in ways that are genuinely at home in the contemporary world. It also respects the diversity evident in the New Testament while taking seriously the fact that generations of Christians (in the tradition) have pondered how to understand God's purposes. It allows that one reader may catch something in the text that another may miss. This approach offers the church a method for dealing with texts that seem to commend ideas and behaviors that may be troubling. New data can more easily be woven into interpreting the text. This approach can lead to correctives in understandings of God that may have been repressive. From time to time, this approach has allowed interpreters to conclude that individual texts in the New Testament may fundamentally misrepresent God.

While I follow this approach myself, I stress its great potential weakness: The church can easily make God into our own image and interpret God's purposes as little more than an extension of our own values. As one of my teachers said, "It can be so easy to tame the New Testament." This approach can also leave people in the congregation unsettled as to what they can count on. I remember a lay person's remark. "For fifty years I believed one thing. Now you're saying I can believe something else. Which is it?"

A Second Way: The Single Voice Speaking Authoritatively

People who view the New Testament as a single voice speaking authoritatively regard the New Testament as their primary resource for understanding God's presence and purposes. They typically believe that God is responsible for the content of the New Testament, although they have many different ways of explaining God's relationship to the creation of the New Testament. Some say that God guided the hands of the writers. Others think that God inspired the general ideas, which writers then put into their own words. But, at the end of the day, the New Testament is reliable because God guided its writing. Human beings may differ with respect to how to understand the meaning or significance of particular passages; in so doing, they differ over how to understand God's direct word for today.

From this point of view, the writings of the New Testament are all internally consistent with one another. While the New Testament writers may use different words or presume different contexts, the overall messages of the different books are all in general agreement. The elements of the New Testament do not disagree with one another.

Furthermore, the message of the New Testament is valid in every time and place. The responsibility of the church is twofold. First, the church must understand the New Testament in its historical context. Second, the church must then apply the religious message of the New Testament to the world today. Of course, the church will sometimes struggle with how to apply the New Testament for today.

Tradition is valuable in this approach when tradition expands or clarifies insights that are in the New Testament itself. When voices in the tradition do not go along with the New Testament, the church should disregard or even criticize those voices.

When experience today is consistent with experience as interpreted in the New Testament, the church can affirm that experience. But when experience today contradicts what is advocated by the New Testament, the church needs to call people to reshape their lives to bring them in line with the New Testament ideal.

In this stream of thought, reason also has a double function. The church uses reason to determine the degree to which voices in the tradition and experience cohere with the New Testament. Christian communities who follow this approach often use reason to show why their understanding of the New Testament is correct and their understanding of God's purposes is convincing. They often seek to prove that their perspective makes sense even in the face of science. When science and the New Testament come into conflict, those affiliated with this approach will redouble their efforts to use reason to demonstrate why the New Testament is believable.

Strengths and Weaknesses

The great strength of this approach is that it is relatively straightforward. When you understand what the New Testament meant in its own context, you have a clear idea of what it means today. Once you understand God's purposes through a text, all you have to do is apply those purposes to today. To be sure, applying the New Testament to specific situations can be challenging, but the challenge is one of working out details rather than wrestling with how to understand God's fundamental purposes. Furthermore, the single-voice model emphasizes that the New Testament as a distinct word given to the church carries much more weight than any culturally bound reflection. By presenting the New Testament as timeless and universal in its validity, this perspective offers congregations a sense of security and continuity. "What was true yesterday is true today, and will be true tomorrow," said a thoughtful minister trained in this approach.

A major potential weakness of the single-voice model is similar to the one I identified in connection with the preceding approach. Those who follow it can easily read their own beliefs into the New Testament without pausing to consider whether those beliefs are inherent in the New Testament itself. Communities of faith in this vein sometimes find themselves in an awkward place when a text appears to go against the grain of contemporary scientific thinking or licenses human behavior that is troubling. There are congregations who advocate behaviors that most people would consider oppressive. Some understandings of God's purposes that flow from this point of view can seem archaic and out of touch today. This position also struggles to harmonize New Testament texts that seem to be in contradiction with each other.

Many Christians Are in the Middle

North Americans like to avoid extremism and to find a middle way. Not surprisingly, my impression is that few Christians are pure representatives of either pole. Many Christians combine elements of these two approaches. But, as a colleague of mine says, people who take this middle route are often susceptible to "picking and choosing what they want to believe." This colleague goes on, "It's like they're picking fruit at the farmer's market. They pick up a piece of fruit and squeeze it, and if they like it they put it in their bags; but if they don't like it, they leave that piece in the back of the truck." Those who want to take a middle way need to be careful to respect the integrity of the New Testament and of their own processes of reasoning.

How Do I Know Where I Fit?

How do you decide which approach to take? A lot of people drift into one approach or the other without consciously making a choice.

They may have grown up in a congregation that moves in one stream and take their approach for granted. If you are new to the church, you may have picked up a view of Christianity without realizing that other approaches exist.

Some people are quite deliberate in naming what they believe. Some have grown uneasy with the approach in which they grew up or that they inherited when they joined the church. I strongly recommend that you think clearly about how you understand God's purposes and consider why you take a particular position. In the end you will want a faith that makes sense to you in the world in which we live. A good approach will make sense and be consistent. A good approach will provide you with purpose and direction, and will give you a framework within which to make difficult decisions. You want to be aware of the strengths and weaknesses of your own interpretive style. Only by examining yourself and your approach with care will you be able to interpret the presence and purposes of the living God.

A Benediction of Love

To be honest, as long as we are in this life we cannot *know* that our understandings of God's purposes are complete. We are finite. We live in a finite world. Only God is infinite. While we wait for final and complete knowledge, we should keep in mind that representatives from each end of the spectrum of interpretation all agree that God is love. The nature of God should determine what happens in the church. We should love one another. Consequently, when people using these different approaches disagree with one another, it should be done with the kind of love that is stronger than any of our differences.

QUESTIONS FOR DISCUSSION

1. Before reading this chapter, how would you have characterized the way you went about identifying God's purposes? Where did you get that approach? From your upbringing? As a result of your religious life? Some other sources?

2. This chapter admits that speaking of *two* basic ways of using the New Testament is an oversimplification. However, making a forced choice sometimes helps us recognize qualities that we most value. Which one of the two basic ways of understanding and using the New Testament do you find most attractive? What do you see as the strengths of that point of view? What do you regard as some weaknesses or dangers?

3. Read Ephesians 5:21-33. How might a person who listens to the single-voice New Testament state God's purposes for the relationship of wives and husbands as found in this text? How might a person who comes to the New Testament with a multi-voice, conversational model use this text in seeking to understand God's purposes in the relationship of husbands and wives?

4. As you reach the end of this book, what have been your most important discoveries? How do you think they will help you?

APPENDIX A

Choosing a Translation of the New Testament

You will need to choose one or more translations of the New Testament for your own reading. The New Testament was originally written in Greek. Scholars have translated the Greek into English. Because the translators can use different English words to translate the same Greek word or phrase, there are many different translations of the New Testament. A translation is never completely neutral nor objective but always reflects some of the translators' biases.

I recommend that you choose a translation with the following characteristics. The translation should be clear and should use language that feels current and well represents the language idioms of our own times. The translation should attempt to honor how people at the time of the first century would have understood the words and ideas in the New Testament and should not impose too many of the translators' own religious beliefs on the text. A good Bible translation should use language for women and men in a way that includes both genders. This latter approach is called "inclusive language"; it particularly avoids masculine language such as "man" and "men" when referring to the human family.

The following are among the most widely used contemporary translations. Many of these translations of the New Testament are actually part of a translation of the whole Bible. I have space to mention only a few of the most widely used translations. You will likely find these translations in many bookstores.

- The *New Revised Standard Version* (abbreviated NRSV) is one of the most popular and well-respected translations. It attempts to translate the text as straightforwardly as possible. It uses quite a bit of inclusive language. This version is the one that I use.
- *New International Version* (NIV) is another of the most popular and well-respected versions. It has gone through a number of revisions, the most recent just having been published in 2011. This version uses some inclusive language. The translators do read some later Christian doctrine into the text of the New Testament.
- *The Message* was translated from the original language by Eugene Peterson. Many Christians love this version because Peterson makes contemporary implications clear. However, in doing so, the translator sometimes overlooks cultural differences between then and now and also reads his own theology into the text.
- The *Good News Translation* (GNT) is a new version of *Today's English Version* (TEV), which is itself an update of *Good News for Modern Man.* This translation is immediately accessible since it uses English at a very basic level.
- For the *Contemporary English Version* (CEV), the translators studied how newspapers, magazines, and the electronic media use speech in order to give the language in this translation a contemporary feel.
- The *New Living Translation* (NLT) is a more scholarly version of the exceptionally popular *The Living Bible.* The latter is not a translation (directly from Greek) but a paraphrase of English translations. However, the *New Living Translation* is an actual translation. The translators have read quite a few later doctrinal formulations into the translation.
- The *Jerusalem Bible* (JB) comes from the Roman Catholic community. The translation is contemporary, lively, and often poetic. Occasionally, Roman Catholic religious thinking shows through.
- The *Revised English Bible* (REB) was made by scholars in the

United Kingdom to update the earlier *New English Bible.* Scholars have great respect for both translations. The wording of the REB sometimes has a British ring.

- The *New King James Version* (NKJV) is an update of the majestic and widely used *King James Version* (KJV). While the New King James has eliminated the "thees" and "thous" of the original KJV, I find it too stilted and convoluted.

The following are among the most reliable electronic sources for Bible study:

- Biblegateway.com: an electronic concordance that searches 100 versions.
- Bibletab.com: an electronic concordance that searches 12 Bible translations.
- Bibleworks provides a variety of resources, such as various translations, concordances, Bible dictionaries, and background studies: http://www.bibleworks.com/. You can search the major translations electronically.
- Olive Tree Bible Software provides materials similar to Bibleworks with apps to a wide variety of platforms: http://www.olivetree.com/.
- For learning the biblical languages, The Gramcord Institute provides material found at http://www.gramcord.org/contents .htm.

Resources for Further Study

When you engage in Bible study either as an individual or as a group, your work will be enriched if you have some resources that delve deeply into the New Testament and its world. It would be good to have at least one book from each of the following groups of resources. I could put many titles under each heading. However, I list only one or two titles that are especially useful to students in the beginning stages of Bible study. Every Bible school class and Bible study group should have these resources in the room when they meet. In lively groups, questions always come up, and it can be very instructive simply to reach for a resource that will provide some answers. You can find many resources on line in each of these categories.

Introduction to the New Testament

When referring to a book, the phrase "Introduction to the New Testament" refers to a book that is similar to *Reading the New Testament for the First Time,* except that it goes into much more detail.

Bart D. Ehrman. *The New Testament: A Historical Introduction to the Early Christian Writings,* 5th ed. (Oxford: Oxford University Press, 2011). This is one of the most popular introductions to the New Testament. In addition to explaining the New Testament, it contains information about other writings from the same time period and excellent photographs.

Dennis Smith, ed. *Chalice Introduction to the New Testament* (St. Louis: Chalice Press, 2004). This volume is unusual in two ways: (1) Whereas most introductions to the New Testament confine themselves to explaining the New Testament in its ancient setting, this one explicitly discusses the meanings of the New Testament books for today. (2) Rather than being written by one or two people, it uses ten different contributors.

Concordance

A concordance gives an alphabetical list of important words in the New Testament and the passages where those words are found. If I want to find a passage that focuses on love, I turn to "love" and note the passages where the word "love" occurs. A concordance is usually keyed to a particular translation, but for most searches you can use a concordance with any translation. A "complete" or "exhaustive" concordance lists every word in the New Testament. One such concordance is Edward W. Goodrick and John R. Kohlenberger III, *Zondervan NIV Exhaustive Concordance* (Grand Rapids: Zondervan, 1999).

Currently there is no exhaustive concordance to the New Revised Standard Version in print. You might find the following useful: John R. Kohlenberger, *Concise Concordance to the New Revised Standard Version* (New York: Oxford University Press, 1993).

Study Bible

A study Bible publishes the text of the Bible, usually on the top half of the page, and furnishes brief explanatory notes, usually on the bottom half of the page. A couple of examples are Harold W. Attridge, ed., *The HarperCollins Study Bible* (San Francisco: HarperCollins, 2006); and Bruce Birch, Brian K. Blount, Thomas G. Long, and Gail R. O'Day, eds., *The Discipleship Study Bible* (Louisville: Westminster John Knox, 2008).

Bible Dictionary

As the name implies, a Bible dictionary discusses important words and concepts, names, places, and the like from the Bible in alphabetical order. Usually such a dictionary traces the original meaning of the subject and how the different biblical writers contribute to its meaning or history. A one-volume Bible dictionary provides a few paragraphs per entry. Multi-volume Bible dictionaries provide pages of information. Here are a few:

Mark Powell, ed. *HarperCollins Bible Dictionary.* Revised edition (San Francisco: HarperCollins, 2011). A one-volume Bible dictionary.

Geoffrey Bromiley, ed. *The International Standard Bible Encyclopedia.* Fully revised (Grand Rapids: Eerdmans, 1988). Four volumes.

David Noel Freedman, Allen C. Myers, and Astrid Beck, eds. *Eerdmans Dictionary of the Bible* (Grand Rapids: Eerdmans, 2000). A one-volume Bible dictionary.

Katherine Doob Sakenfeld, ed. *The New Interpreter's Dictionary of the Bible* (Nashville: Abingdon, 2006-2009). Five volumes.

Bible Commentary

Among Bible students, the word "commentary" refers to a work that provides a detailed explanation of each passage in the New Testament. A commentary explains such things as the historical background, the meaning of words, the literary style, and what the reader ought to take away. A one-volume commentary provides a compact version of such information. Larger commentaries devote one or more volume to a single book in the New Testament. A few of them are listed below.

James D. G. Dunn and John Rogerson, eds. *Eerdmans Commentary on the Bible* (Grand Rapids: Eerdmans, 2003). A one-volume commentary on the whole Bible.

Interpretation: A Bible Commentary for Preaching and Teaching (Louisville: Westminster John Knox, 1982ff.). 43 volumes, most of them focusing on one book in the Bible. The volumes in the series comment on the meaning of texts in their historical setting and suggest possible meanings for today.

Leander Keck, ed. *The New Interpreter's Bible* (Nashville: Abingdon, 1994ff.). Twelve volumes. This series offers extensive historical explanations on each biblical text, plus comments on the significance of the texts for today.

James L. Mays, ed. *HarperCollins Bible Commentary.* Revised edition (San Francisco: HarperCollins, 2000). A one-volume commentary on the whole Bible.

Three Plans for Reading through the Entire New Testament

You will benefit from reading books about the New Testament, such as *Reading the New Testament for the First Time* and the books listed in Appendix B. But there is no substitute for reading the New Testament itself. Over many centuries and in many different contexts, the words of the New Testament have shown their power to transform lives.

This appendix offers three plans for reading the entire New Testament. The first plan is simply to read the books of the New Testament in order. The second plan is to read the books of the New Testament in the order in which they were written (following the chronology in Chapter 3). The third plan is to read the books (or parts of books) of the New Testament in the order of the events recounted in the New Testament (following the outline of Chapters 3 through 9). Alternately, you may find a plan for reading the New Testament published by your congregation or denomination or in some other place, such as a devotional book. There are many plans for making your way through the Bible. The important thing is to get into the New Testament itself.

In the case of each plan, I have listed books (or parts of books) in the order in which to read them. To save space, I have not given specific Bible readings for each day. You can set out a reading schedule according to your own reading style and preferences.

Some readers like to dive into a book of the Bible and continue reading until they finish. It takes a typical reader about three hours to read the longer books (such as Matthew, Luke, John, Romans, the Corinthian letters, Hebrews, and the book of Revelation). If you like this pattern of reading, perhaps you could read a book every Saturday morning. In only six months, you would finish the New Testament.

Other readers like to read a part of a book each day. If you are one of these people, you might like to know that the New Testament contains 260 chapters. It takes about fifteen minutes to read a chapter. Almost everyone can find fifteen minutes for reading at the beginning or end of the day (or perhaps at lunchtime). If you read fifteen minutes (one chapter) every day, you will finish the New Testament in just under nine months.

When reading the books of the New Testament, it might be a good refresher to review the sections of *Reading the New Testament for the First Time* that correlate with the part you are reading. For example, when reading the book of Romans, you might read the section on Romans to provide a little historical context for the biblical material.

Plan 1: Reading the Books of the New Testament in Their Present Order

The first plan is simply to read the books of the New Testament in their present order. You simply start reading with the Gospel of Matthew and make your way to the book of Revelation. This approach has the advantage of exposing you to the books of the New Testament in the approximate order of the major events in the New Testament (though I propose a more detailed Plan 3 along these lines). It begins with the story of Jesus in the Gospels, followed by the story of the early church in the first half of Acts, then the story of Paul in the latter part of Acts and in Paul's own letters. This approach does break down in the latter part of the New Testament when books from different authors and contexts sit alongside each other.

Plan 2: Reading the Books in the Order
in Which They Were Written

In this plan you read the books of the New Testament in the order in which they were written. This chronology is set out in Chapter 3.

1 Thessalonians
Galatians
1 Corinthians
2 Corinthians
Philippians
Philemon
Romans
Colossians
Mark
Matthew
Luke-Acts
1 Peter
James
Ephesians
Jude
John
2 Thessalonians
2 Peter
Revelation
Hebrews
1 Timothy
2 Timothy
Titus
1 John
2 John
3 John

Plan 3: Reading the New Testament in the Order of the Chronology of Events

I hesitate to recommend this plan (see Box 34, p. 192) because it cuts passages out of the specific books in which they are found and pastes them into a chronological order for which their authors did not intend them. This approach risks violating the integrity of biblical books or a biblical author. Nevertheless, this approach is how many Christians have viewed the relationship between the events of the New Testament and the books that tell about them. This plan follows the approximate chronology of events in Chapter 3. If you follow this approach, I urge you to respect the particularity of the individual books of the New Testament as they interpret these events. When reading about similar events in different books, you could note how each author tells the story a little differently.

To read about the ministry of Jesus, I recommend that you purchase (or check out from a library) a copy of a synopsis. A synopsis is a book that prints the Gospels in parallel columns: Matthew, Mark, Luke, and John. That way you can quickly compare and contrast how the different writers present the different incidents and sayings. The best synopsis is Kurt Aland, *Synopsis of the Four Gospels* (Peabody, Mass.: Hendrickson, 2006). You could read one, two, three (or more) sections in the synopsis each day. In just a few weeks, you would have read the story of Jesus following the chronological order of the Gospel writers and in such a way that you could hear each writer's distinctive telling.

The book of Acts divides nicely into reading segments. You can correlate some readings from Paul's own letters with your reading through Acts.

For the story of the early church after the resurrection and ascension until the narrative of the ministry of Paul, see Acts 1:1–12:25. Important subsections include Acts 1:1-26, Jesus' ascension and choosing an apostle to replace Judas; Acts 2:1-42, the coming of the Spirit on the Day of Pentecost (with which you might read John 20:19-23); Acts 3:1–4:31, the healing of a person at the Gate Beautiful and its aftermath; Acts 4:32–6:7, more healings, more controversy, and the election of the first deacons; Acts 6:8–8:1, the stoning of Stephen (the first martyr); Acts 8:2-40, the gospel goes into Samaria and takes steps out of Judea toward the ends of the earth.

Luke gives his version of Paul's call in Acts 9:1-30, while Paul gives his own narration in Galatians 1:11-17. With Acts 13:1, the story of Paul's ministry takes center stage for the rest of the book of Acts.

Luke reports the early phase of Paul's ministry in Acts 13:1–14:28, while Paul comments on a similar period in Galatians 1:18-24.

Luke interprets the Jerusalem Conference, which was pivotal for Paul's ministry and the life of the early church, in Acts 15:1-35, while Paul interprets the same event in Galatians 2:1-10. Note, too, Paul's description of a follow-up event at Antioch in Galatians 2:11-21.

From Acts 15:36 to 18:17, Luke offers a rendition of Paul's missionary journey to Philippi (Acts 16:11-40), Thessalonica (Acts 17:1-15), Athens (Acts 17:14), and Corinth (Acts 18:1-17). Since Paul wrote 1 Thessalonians while staying in Corinth, you could read that letter here. And since Paul wrote 1 Corinthians during his time in Ephesus (Acts 18:18-19:41), you might read 1 Thessalonians in connection with Ephesus. Paul likely wrote Galatians about this time.

Paul also wrote 2 Corinthians during this general period, but in a different order from which the parts of 2 Corinthians appear in the Bible. You might read them in the order that some scholars think is most likely. (a) 2 Corinthians 6:14–7:1 is a fragment of a letter written before tension erupted between the Corinthians and Paul; (b) 2 Corinthians 10:1–13:10 is a letter in which Paul defends himself against charges made against him in Corinth; (c) 2 Corinthians 1:3–6:13; 7:2-16 is a letter seeking reconciliation between the apostle and the congregation. (d) 2 Corinthians 8:1–9:15 is a letter calling for the Corinthians to collect an offering for the church in Jerusalem.

Paul's letter to the Philippians was written when the apostle was imprisoned, but it does not indicate which imprisonment. You could read Philippians in connection with any of the three times Acts mentions Paul in prison: Acts 16:23-40, Acts 23:23-26:32, or Acts 28:16-31. The same is true of Philemon: Paul wrote it from prison but does not indicate where.

Acts 21:1-26 recounts Paul's return to Jerusalem. In Acts 21:27-36, Luke tells about Paul's arrest by the Roman authorities, which marks the beginning of his journey to Rome. Luke tells this story in phases. The hearings in Jerusalem are described in Acts 21:37–23:11. Paul is taken under guard to Caesarea and interrogated there (Acts 23:23–26:32). Finally, Paul journeyed to Rome (including being shipwrecked), where he was held under house arrest and executed (Acts 27:1–28:31).

It would now be natural to read the letters attributed to Paul. That would give you a sense of how some people in the early church interpreted Paul: Colossians, Ephesians, 2 Thessalonians, 1 Timothy, 2 Timothy, and Titus.

Several of the remaining letters deal in a central way with the Second Coming and the importance of the church being prepared for that event while continuing to live faithfully in the world: 1 Peter, James, Jude, 2 Peter, and the book of Revelation.

The book of Hebrews is a sermon. When reading it, you might imagine yourself being addressed by a preacher.

As noted when we discussed 1, 2, and 3 John, these letters have a sectarian character. However, their teaching on God as love and on the importance of loving one another would be an appropriate conclusion to reading the New Testament. If God is truly love, then the command to love other church members can easily be extended to love for the whole human family and for the natural world.

Box 34. Chart for Reading the New Testament in the Order of the Chronology of Events

Because of limitations of space, a number of these readings are given in large blocks of material. You may want to break them into smaller units. As indicated in the main body of the chapter, a synopsis (a book that prints the texts of Matthew, Mark, Luke, and John in parallel columns) can be your best friend when reading the story of Jesus. Most scholars today believe that the chronology of Jesus' ministry in Matthew, Mark, and Luke is different from the sequence of events in John. Nevertheless, for purposes of comparison, readings from John are given in the chronology below.

An alternate approach to reading the story of Jesus would be to read Matthew, Mark, and Luke together, and then to read the Gospel of John separately. You could then proceed to Acts.

Events in the New Testament in Chronological Order	Passages to Read from the New Testament	Notes on the Readings	Pages above Where This Material Is Discussed
Jesus before the New Testament: a hymn of theological reflection on Jesus' significance	John 1:1-18	Note that John does not have a conventional birth story but begins by offering a distinctive interpretation of Jesus as the Word descended from heaven.	pp. 114-16
Birth of John the Baptist and Jesus	Matthew 1:1–2:23 Luke 1:1–2:52	Note the differences between the birth stories in Matthew and in Luke.	pp. 39-40, 57, 145-47
Preaching of John the Baptist	Matthew 3:1-12 Mark 1:1-8 Luke 3:1-20 John 1:6-8, 19-34	Note the different nuances in the picture of John the Baptist in the first three Gospels and in the Gospel of John.	pp. 39-40, 57
Jesus' baptism, temptation, and the first words of Jesus' public ministry	Matthew 3:13–4:17 Mark 1:9-15 Luke 3:21-22; 4:1-30	In each Gospel, note the differences in the first words that Jesus speaks and in the temptations.	pp. 39-40, 57-58

Call of the first disciples	Matthew 4:18-22 Mark 1:16-20 Luke 5:1-11 John 1:35-51	Note the similarities in Matthew/Mark and the distinctive elements in Luke and John.	pp. 40, 57-58, 68-69
Beginning of Jesus' ministry in Galilee	Matthew 4:23-25 Mark 1:21-3:19a Luke 5:12-6:16		pp. 57-58
Sermon on the Mount and Sermon on the Plain	Matthew 5:1-7:29 Luke 6:17-49	Compare these two versions of similar sermonic material.	pp. 58-60, 155-56
Beginning of Jesus' public ministry in John	John 1:35-3:36	How do Jesus' activities differ in this part of John from Matthew, Mark, and Luke? Note, especially, that Jesus arrives in Jerusalem in John 2:13 with much less fanfare than in the first three Gospels (Matthew 21:1-9; Mark 11:1-10; Luke 19:28-40). Note how early the cleansing of the temple comes in John (2:14-22). Also note that John has little material about Jesus' Galilean ministry.	pp. 114-16, 117, 154
Jesus' ministry continues in Galilee.	Matthew 8:1-16:12 Mark 4:1-8:26 Luke 7:1-9:17	You may want to read this long body of material in bits and pieces over several days.	pp. 60-62, 157-60, 161-62
Peter's confession of Jesus as Messiah, Jesus' teaching that the way of the Messiah and the disciples is the way of suffering, and confirmation at the Transfiguration	Matthew 16:13-17:13 Mark 8:27-9:13 Luke 9:18-36	This material is so important that it deserves careful reading.	pp. 60-62
Continuation of Jesus' ministry in Galilee	Matthew 17:14-18:35 Mark 9:14-50 Luke 9:37-50	Note, especially, Matthew's distinctive material in 18:1-35.	pp. 60-62
Jesus ministers in Galilee in John.	John 4:43-54		pp. 114-16, 117

Jesus' journey from Galilee to Jerusalem	Matthew 19:1-34 Mark 10:1-52 Luke 9:51–19:27	Note the distinctiveness of Luke's extended narrative of the journey to Jerusalem.	pp. 60-62
Jesus returns from Galilee to Jerusalem in John.	John 5:1-47		pp. 114-16, 117
Jesus goes back to Galilee in John.	John 6:1–7:1		pp. 114-16, 117
Jesus goes to Jerusalem and has conflicts with the authorities in John.	John 7:2–10:42		pp. 114-16, 117
Jesus goes to Bethany (outside of Jerusalem) and raises Lazarus in John.	John 11:1–12:11		pp. 114-16, 117
Jesus enters Jerusalem.	Matthew 21:1-9 Mark 11:1-10 Luke 19:28-40 John 12:12-19	Although the church typically calls this event "Palm Sunday," note that "palms" appear only in John.	p. 117
Jesus' ministry in Jerusalem	Matthew 21:10–23:39 Mark 11:11–12:44 Luke 19:41–21:4		pp. 62-63
Jesus' final teaching: the focus is the end.	Matthew 24:1–25:46 Mark 13:1-37 Luke 21:5-38	Note Matthew's distinctive material in 24:37–25:46.	pp. 62-63
Jesus' final ministry in Jerusalem in John (sometimes called the farewell discourses)	John 12:20–17:26	Note the many familiar themes in this distinctively Johannine material.	pp. 114-15, 117
Jesus' last days: last supper, betrayal, trial	Matthew 26:1–27:31 Mark 14:1–15:20 Luke 22:1–23:25 John 18:1–19:16a	Note both similarities and differences between these accounts of Jesus' last days.	pp. 74-75, 117
Within Jesus' last days, note the institution of the Lord's Supper.	Matthew 26:17-29 Mark 14:12-25 Luke 22:7-20	Compare the words that Jesus speaks at the last supper. Note that John does not have a distinct recollection of this meal, but see John 6:1-65.	pp. 74-75

Jesus washes the disciples' feet.	John 13:1-20	This event occurs only in John in the larger context of John 12:20–17:26.	pp. 114-15, 117
The death and burial of Jesus	Matthew 27:32-66 Mark 15:21-47 Luke 23:26-56 John 19:16b-42	Note elements particular to each Gospel in these accounts.	pp. 62-63, 117
The first reports of Jesus' resurrection, and his resurrected appearance	Matthew 28:1-15 Mark 16:1-8 Luke 24:1-12 John 20:1-18	Compare these different stories, especially noting the roles of the women.	pp. 41, 117
Further reports of Jesus' resurrection	Luke 24:13-43 John 20:19-29	Note the distinctive elements in each account.	pp. 41, 117
Jesus' climactic words	Matthew 28:16-20 Luke 24:44-49 John 21:1-25	Note how Jesus describes the mission of the disciples in each Gospel.	pp. 41, 117
Jesus ascends to heaven.	Luke 24:50-53 Acts 1:1-11	Although only Luke describes this event, many New Testament authors assume it.	pp. 41, 63-64
Waiting for Pentecost	Acts 1:12-26		pp. 42, 72-73
Pentecost (the coming of the Holy Spirit on Jewish believers)	Acts 2:1-42	Compare this passage with John 20:19-23.	pp. 42, 72-73
The witness of the church after Pentecost in Jerusalem, Judea, and Samaria	Acts 2:43–8:40	Note how the movement from Jerusalem through Judea to Samaria fulfills Acts 1:8.	pp. 42-43, 71-72
The call of Saul (Paul) and his early witness in Jerusalem	Acts 9:1-30	Compare this account with Acts 22:6-21 and Acts 26:12-23, and especially with Paul's own report in Galatians 1:11-24.	pp. 43, 70-77, 83-87
The witness of the church continues.	Acts 9:31–12:24	Acts 10:34-48 is sometimes called the "gentile Pentecost."	pp. 87-88

Paul's first missionary journey	Acts 13:1–14:27	While Paul himself does not speak of three distinct missionary journeys, you might note Paul's own account of a similar period in Galatians 1:18-24.	pp. 44, 87-88, map p. 89
The council at Jerusalem	Acts 15:1-35	Compare this passage with Paul's account in Galatians 2:1-21.	pp. 43, 87-88
Paul's second missionary journey	Acts 15:36–18:22	Acts depicts Paul passing through Galatia in Acts 16:6 and 18:23. You might, then, read	pp. 44, 87-88, map p. 89
	Galatians	Galatians here. Acts depicts Paul in Thessalonica in Acts 17:9; you could	pp. 48, 97-98
	1 Thessalonians	read 1 Thessalonians here. Acts depicts Paul in Corinth in Acts 18:1-17; consequently, you might	pp. 48, 96-97
	1 and 2 Corinthians	read 1 and 2 Corinthians here. When reading Paul's own letters in relation to Acts, it is important to remember that Acts and Paul's letters are from different authors and deal with different issues.	pp. 48, 98-100
Paul's third missionary journey	Acts 18:23–20:38		p. 44, map p. 89
Paul's journey to Jerusalem	Acts 21:1-16		p. 44, map p. 89
Paul in Jerusalem	Acts 21:17–23:22		p. 44, map p. 89

Paul in Caesarea on the sea	Acts 23:23–26:32	Paul wrote Philippians while imprisoned, but does not indicate a partic- ular imprisonment. You might, then, read	p. 44, map p. 89
	Philippians	Philippians in connection with Acts 23:23–26:32 or with one of Paul's other incarcerations in Acts. The	pp. 48, 100-109
	Philemon	same is true of Philemon: it was written during an imprisonment not corre- lated with an incident in Acts, but you could read it in connection with any of Paul's incarcerations in Acts. Most scholars think	pp. 48, 101
	Romans	that Paul wrote Romans prior to his visit to Rome. Although there is no real connection between Acts 23:23–26:32 and Romans, you might read Romans here.	pp. 48, 101-3
Paul sails for Rome, and his ship wrecks.	Acts 27:1–28:10		p. 44, map p. 89
Paul is in prison in Rome.	Acts 28:11-31	Although Luke does not directly report that Rome executed Paul, Luke has prepared the reader to conclude that the Romans put Paul to death (Acts 9:16; 19:21; 20:22-25; 21:10-14; 23:11; 26:32; 27:23-25).	p. 44, map p. 89
If you did not read Paul's seven letters in relation to Acts, this would be a good place to read them.	1 Thessalonians Galatians 1 Corinthians 2 Corinthians Philippians Philemon Romans	This listing is in the order in which these letters were likely written. Can you get a feel for how Paul's thought emerged and evolved?	p. 48

Colossians	Since Colossians might have been written by one of Paul's followers, you might look for continuities with and differences from Paul.	pp. 49, 123-24
1 Peter	The author of 1 Peter writes to a community who perceive themselves as exiles or outsiders. You might try to read this book as if you are an exile or outsider.	pp. 51, 133-35
James	Some Christians have said that James is not a very good book because it teaches works-righteousness, that is, the idea that we have to engage in certain works in order to earn God's grace. More recently, increasing numbers of Christians see James calling for works as a faithful response to God's grace. As you read James, how do you come down on this issue?	pp. 51, 132-33
Ephesians	See the note on Colossians above. In addition, you could read Ephesians with an eye toward similarities to and differences from Paul and Colossians.	pp. 51, 124-25
Jude	Many scholars think that Jude and 2 Peter are closely related. You might read these books noting points of similarity and difference.	pp. 51, 135-36
2 Thessalonians	What points of comparison and contrast do you note between 1 and 2 Thessalonians?	p. 51

2 Peter	See the note on Jude above.	pp. 52, 135-36
Revelation	Because this book places such a big role in end-times discussions today, people often think they know more about it than they actually do. I recommend that before attempting to apply the message of Revelation to today, you try as hard as you can to simply read it on its own. Try to get a sense for what is actually in (or not in) the book.	pp. 52, 136-38, 162-63
Hebrews	Since many interpreters think that this book was an early Christian sermon, you might read it as if you are hearing it in worship.	pp. 52, 130-31
1 Timothy	See the note on Colossians above. In addition, you could read 1 and 2 Timothy and Titus with an eye toward similarities to and differences from Paul's letters as well as Colossians and Ephesians.	pp. 52, 127
2 Timothy	In addition to the preceding note, you might look at 2 Timothy with an eye toward similarities to and differences from 1 Timothy.	pp. 52, 127
Titus	In addition to the preceding note, you might look at Titus with an eye toward similarities to and differences from 1 and 2 Timothy.	pp. 52, 127

1 John	Most scholars think that the three letters of John share much of the same worldview as the Gospel of John. What similarities and differences do you notice between these letters and the Gospel of John?	pp. 52, 131-32
2 John		pp. 52, 131-32
3 John		pp. 52, 131-32

The Names "Old Testament" and "New Testament"

Ironically, the names "Old Testament" and "New Testament" never occur in the Bible itself to refer to the thirty-nine or more books (old) or the twenty-seven books (new) that bear those names today. Church leaders imposed these designations in the second century C.E. Prior to that time, Christians spoke more simply about "the scriptures" and referred to specific books and passages.

The first recorded use of the expression "Old Testament" is found in the writings of a Christian preacher named Melito of Sardis in 180 C.E.; he used the phrase "Old Testament" to criticize Jewish beliefs and to indicate the inferiority of the Old Testament. About the same time, another Christian leader, Irenaeus (pronounced "Eye-re-KNEE-us"), gave us the first recorded use of the term "New Testament." Irenaeus also used the term "Old Testament" but was much more positive than Melito about Judaism.

In general English usage, in the context of a "last will and testament," the word "testament" indicates a document that directs the distribution of a person's estate after death. In Christian circles, the word "testament" often refers to a covenant (or promise or agreement) between God and human beings.

In the chronological sense, the "Old Testament" refers to the original revelation of God's promise to and through the people of Israel. The "New Testament" tells the story of God re-presenting that promise through Jesus Christ.

Many Christians today recognize that the term "old" has a negative connotation (for example, inferior, out of date, worn out), whereas the word "new" indicates something that is improved and superior.[1] Using the words "Old Testament" and "New Testament," then, can imply that the Old Testament is second rate, even harmful, while the New and Improved Testament has replaced the Old. Most scholars today believe that this way of thinking is not only incorrect but contributes to anti-Semitism.

For the sake of familiarity, I use the terms "Old Testament" and "New Testament" in this book. But many Christians are using new terminology for these parts of the Bible, such as First Testament and Second Testament, Hebrew Bible, or Hebrew Scriptures (since most of the Old Testament was originally in Hebrew). I prefer to speak of the different parts of the Bible as Torah (Law), Prophets, Writings, Gospels, and Letters.

---

1. This usage is quite different from that of antiquity. In the ancient world, people often valued old things.